The Debt of Nations

A Twentieth Century Fund Paper

THE DEBT OF NATIONS

BY M. S. MENDELSOHN

Priority Press Publications/New York/1984

The Twentieth Century Fund is an independent research foundation which undertakes policy studies of economic, political, and social institutions and issues. The Fund was founded in 1919 and endowed by Edward A. Filene.

Manufactured in the United States of America.
ISBN: 0-87078-158-8

Foreword

Many different groups, public and private, have been pondering the threat to the world's financial system posed by the excessive indebtedness of the developing countries. Most of the proposals put forth by these groups have been either highly technical or exercises in self-interest. Very few of them have taken into account the political pressures that complicate the search for solutions. Official groups are inhibited in their consideration of political forces, while private authorities have, for the most part, concentrated on economic or financial questions.

The avoidance or neglect of political issues presented an opportunity for the Twentieth Century Fund. Since the Fund does not believe there is any simple or single solution, we have devoted a portion of our resources to a number of different projects, ranging from book-length studies to monographs. So far, we have published *Deficits and Detente,* a Report of a Conference jointly sponsored by Geneva's Center for Research on International Institutions and its Graduate Institute of International Studies and by the Fund, which examined the debts of the Soviet Union and its Comecon allies; and *Next Steps for Summitry,* the Report of an International Conference held last spring, which pointed out that the annual summits are not the appropriate forums for dealing with the specifics of the international debt crisis but could be useful in overcoming institutional and political resistance to suggested reforms. Earlier, of course, we had sponsored *Quest for World Monetary Order,* the late Milton Gilbert's authoritative study of the Bretton Woods system and its breakdown.

Now we have a third publication, a paper that analyzes the current debt situation and places it in a historic perspective. It is the work of Stefan Mendelsohn, special consultant to the World Bank, consultant to the Group of Thirty, associate editor of *The Banker* of London, and European correspondent of the *American Banker.*

Mendelsohn's essay on international debt is a fresh and provocative look at the debt situation. It challenges many of the prevailing assumptions—at least in the United States—that both the banks and the developing countries were deliberately engaging in questionable if not nefarious practices. We think it makes a useful contribution to the debate. We also are confident that other projects that we are supporting will be as informative and as constructive.

M. J. Rossant, DIRECTOR
The Twentieth Century Fund
August 1984

Contents

For

K.M.

Introduction

Why did our banks lend so much to foreign countries, how will the countries repay, and what happens if they cannot or do not?

These questions have preoccupied governments, the financial community, and a concerned public since the late summer of 1982, when one after another more than thirty developing and East European countries suspended interest and principal payments due on about $120 billion of external debt, owed mostly to Western commercial banks.

The questions are fundamental and legitimate. They are posed starkly here, because that is how they are usually addressed in public debate. That form of presentation, however, embodies, at least in part, a precommercial view of debt. It is a view represented in literature by Shakespeare's Polonius, who disapproved of borrowers and lenders alike, and by Charles Dickens's Mr. Micawber, who lived always above his means, hoping that "something" would turn up. Polonius abstained and Micawber succumbed, but they were united in their belief that borrowed money would not be repaid because it would surely be frittered away.

However, this study starts from the different premise that borrowing for profitable investment is essential for the growth of companies and countries alike. Of course borrowers are expected to service individual loans on the terms agreed upon at the start, but the process of running down existing debt and replacing it with new loans is a continuous one. Companies do not normally "pay back" their total outstanding debt unless they go bankrupt or are dissolved for some other reason. Countries do not ordinarily "repay" their total debt either. Unlike companies, they cannot be wound up for creditors. But if their economic development succeeds, they gradually become net lenders to the world, instead of net borrowers.

The underlying argument is that it is right and proper for countries to borrow abroad to supplement domestic savings in order to finance their economic development. Moreover, the thesis that, as more countries prosper, all will eventually benefit has been an underlying tenet of Western policy since the end of World War II, and the current debt problems of some developing countries provide no reason for giving up that belief.

In the continuum of international lending, creditors and borrowers are united by common interests that outweigh their differences, even when they encounter difficulties. That is especially true of sovereign borrowers. The World Bank has likened the relation between them and their creditors to that of partners in a three-legged race, who can walk, limp, or fall together, but who cannot part company.*

Conflicts of interest within and between societies, sharpened by a changing world economy, lie at the heart of the world's present economic difficulties, which have been accumulating for some twenty years. The debt-servicing problems that some developing countries have been experiencing since mid-1982 are only one manifestation of the world's economic problems and by no means the most important. From the late 1960s until the unexpectedly severe three-year global disinflation initiated by the Federal Reserve System in 1979, the economically advanced developing countries and newer industrialized countries achieved very rapid rates of export-led real economic growth by borrowing heavily. Indeed, the rapid growth of their exports threatened many established industries in the mature, industrialized economies.

However, stagnation and at times an actual fall in the volume of world trade during the three years from 1979 to 1982, accompanied by steeply rising real and nominal interest rates, put very heavy pressure on sovereign and corporate borrowers, as well as on the international banking system, which found itself tiding a growing number of countries and companies through their difficulties. It follows that creditors and borrowers depend, above all, on a resumption of stable world economic growth for a return to full debt service and credit standing.

This thesis of overriding shared interests, however, does not imply that the problem will resolve itself. On the contrary, some debtor countries may take years to return to full external debt service and credit standing. Quite possibly, some external debt may eventually be written off. And although far less likely, international creditors may call some countries into formal default. At the extreme, even outright repudiation by one or more developing countries cannot be ruled out, if only on the principle that no eventuality can ever be wholly excluded.

The often untidy, continuing process by which countries and their creditors grope toward a reconciliation of their differences in a framework of strongly shared interests is the focus of this study. The governments of creditor and debtor countries and international commercial banks all contributed to the present difficulty, and all have a stake in its orderly resolution.

**Debt and the Developing World* (Washington, D.C.: International Bank for Reconstruction and Development, January 1984).

This is not intended as a cavalier dismissal of serious critics who complain that some banks acted with insufficient caution and that borrowing countries wasted at least some of the proceeds. There can be no denying inefficiencies at the all-important margin. Some countries did spend far too heavily on consumption, especially some large oil producers such as Mexico and Nigeria, which assumed that oil prices were peculiarly immune from erosion. And some banks did act imprudently, partly by assessing country risk in isolation rather than in the wider context of regional and global economic trends.

Yet such inefficiencies at the margin are a part of any market. If all market participants thought alike, no market would exist, and if all banks lent only to the bluest of blue-chip borrowers, the world economy would grind to a halt. Risk is part of life. "Nothing ventured, nothing gained," goes the adage. And a careful examination of the situation supports the belief that borrowing countries and their creditors, on balance, did not take unacceptable risks.

This examination begins by putting into perspective the size of the present sovereign debt problem. It then goes on to describe by way of background how the world's economic difficulties accumulated from the mid-1960s. It also looks at the important transition from the pegged exchange rates of the Bretton Woods system to the floating exchange rates of the past dozen years.

The relevance of the foreign exchange regime is that, although floating rates were the norm during most of the world's history, they were a novelty to the post-1971 generation. Exchange rates had been stabilized for thirty years, first by controls during and after World War II, and then under Bretton Woods. As a result, it took time for policymakers and bankers to read the different kinds of signals transmitted by floating exchange rates. The widespread assumption that floating exchange rates would automatically correct a country's external financial balance, making other action unnecessary, has been brutally disproved, for developing countries and even for mature industrialized countries like the United States, but it took time for that message to sink in.

The description of exchange rate regimes is a necessary digression because wider exchange rate fluctuations have been accompanied by wider interest rate movements. At root, those wider fluctuations have been one expression of wide shifts in economic policies, especially in the leading industrial countries. Both exchange and interest rate movements have reinforced underlying instability and, therefore, have influenced the way country debt built up during the 1960s and 1970s. In due course, those fluctuations contributed to the debt-servicing difficulties that emerged in a concentrated form in the summer of 1982.

1 • The size of the problem

The spate of international debt renegotiations that began in August 1982 seemed to vindicate many critics who had warned during the 1970s that developing countries were borrowing too much and that commercial banks were lending to them imprudently. Many more observers, employing hindsight, have since come to the same conclusion, although not necessarily for the right reasons. It is certainly true that there has been no recent precedent for the sums at stake, and none for the number of countries involved. The only comparable event occurred more than fifty years ago, in 1931, when Germany, Austria, and several East European and Latin American countries renegotiated terms on the present equivalent of more than $80 billion owed to official and private creditors, mostly in the United States, Britain, the Netherlands, and Switzerland.

Many commentators on the present debt difficulties have suggested, or at least implied, that borrowing by developing countries is a recent phenomenon, that it is intrinsically unsound, that banks lent recklessly to developing countries after the 1973 "oil shock," and that the countries wasted the proceeds. It is impossible not to detect in all this a thinly disguised xenophobia, perhaps even racism, tinged with a certain pleasurable satisfaction that matters have apparently and predictably gone wrong.

Yet the recycling of oil surpluses to deficit countries in the industrialized and developing worlds was novel only for the enlarged role of the international banking system. In the case of developing countries, commercial banks came to play a relatively bigger role in the classical process of countries supplementing domestic savings with imported capital to finance economic growth until they join the ranks of net capital exporting countries, a transition that was made within living memory even by some of today's richest countries. Moreover, the same transfer of savings takes place (in an unrecorded way) between richer and poorer regions within sovereign states, as well as between countries.

So far from squandering the capital they borrowed during the 1970s, the advanced developing countries responsible for the bulk of international borrowing used most of the money wisely and productively. Taken as a group, they achieved an impressive record of export-led growth by concentrating much of their investment in ways that increased their net foreign exchange earnings faster than their debt service, as pointed out by the World Bank in "an unfashionably positive view of the external indebtedness of developing countries."*

Yet the successful use of borrowed capital made by advanced developing countries during the 1970s caused almost as much concern as the more recent suspension of full debt service by some of them. The new challenge created for mature industrial countries, and especially their declining industries, by the growth of competition for world export markets from newer industrialized countries and advanced developing countries partly explains what seems to be a widespread, covert pleasure at the present plight of some developing countries and their bankers.

For the most part, foreign debt taken on at minimal or negative interest rates in the 1970s seemed manageable to the countries and their creditors, and actually was in the circumstances in which the debt was contracted. But hardly anyone foresaw the severity of the three-year global disinflation that began in 1979 and which became the single most important cause for the difficulties of sovereign and corporate borrowers. Even more important was the undue emphasis placed by the leading industrial countries on monetary restraint, which steeply increased the real cost of credit for all borrowers, while severely restricting the ability of companies and countries to earn enough for the maintenance of full debt service.

The plight of some sovereign borrowers is only one symptom of the economic difficulties from which the world has only just begun an uncertain recovery. In classical fashion, debt difficulties peaked at the tail end of the world's latest recession, with record bankruptcies among companies in the industrial world and a concentration of sovereign debt restructurings. In the United States alone, about 52,000 companies went bankrupt in 1982, and a large part of their assets disappeared with them. By contrast, the only significant sovereign debt repudiations of the twentieth century have been on the part of two countries that chose to withdraw from the world community or felt excluded from it for a time, namely, Russia after 1917 and China after 1949.

Unless countries are willing to face the extreme costs of retreating into themselves, they have no alternative to adjustment once they are no longer able to service their foreign debt in full. In plain language, they are forced to increase their export earnings or to cut their spending on imports or to resort to some combination of the two. At the same time, debtor countries and their creditors depend on a sustained expan-

---

**World Debt Tables 1982-1983* (Washington, D.C.: International Bank for Reconstruction and Development, February 1983).

sion of the world's leading economies for an orderly return to full debt service and credit standing. At the extremes, the world economy will collapse or it will not. The default of some developing countries might at worst trigger such an outcome, but would not be its cause. The total of international debt that was not being fully serviced at the end of 1983 amounted to less than 5 percent of the world banking system's total assets.* Its importance lies at that critical margin where the weight of any final straw is, in itself, insignificant by definition.

Present events can readily be put into perspective. Of about eighty international debt-relief agreements signed in the twenty-five years before 1982, nearly seventy covered debt owed by the governments of developing countries to governments of the leading industrial countries. The amounts were small for the creditors, although not, of course, for the debtors. The same was true of the relatively few relief agreements signed with commercial banks during that period. The only exceptions were Turkey, which renegotiated $3 billion of debt owed to the international financial markets in 1979, and Poland, which restructured $4.8 billion in 1982. The international debt restructured or renegotiated between mid-1982 and mid-1984 was therefore about twenty-five times larger than the sum renegotiated in any single year in the course of the previous half-century (namely, about $5 billion in 1981 and early 1982).

Recent debt problems have been highly concentrated among a relative handful of countries. Of the total international debt being restructured

*The exposure of some of the world's biggest international banks is, of course, larger. According to the Federal Reserve *Bulletin* of September 1983 (page 667), the claims of America's nine biggest banks on non-OPEC developing countries rose from 8 to 11 percent of total assets in the five years through 1982. This is similar to the ratio of such claims of larger British and European banks. However, most of their provisions against bad and doubtful debt have been related to lending within the mature industrialized countries, especially their own. Striking examples were the losses incurred by Chase Manhattan in 1982 from the failure of Penn Square Bank in Oklahoma, the Midland Bank's heavy 1983 provisions against losses on California real estate incurred by Crocker National Bank, which the Midland partly owns, and the rescue of Continental Illinois by agencies of the U.S. government in 1984, following years of imprudent domestic lending by America's eighth-biggest bank. About fifty banks failed in the United States in 1983 and the first half of 1984, all as a result of bad domestic lending. Banks do not publish their general and specific provisions in a way that identifies individual borrowers or even classes of borrowers so that there are no statistics on the proportion of provisions and write-offs related to developing-country lending. There is general agreement among bankers and supervisors, however, that the proportion is relatively small.

in 1982–84, a third consisted of the debt of a single country, Mexico; half was owed by two countries, Mexico and Venezuela; and three-quarters of the total was accounted for by five countries, the others being Brazil, Argentina, and Poland (Table 1, page 59). Soaring real interest rates coupled with stagnation and a decline of world trade from 1979 to 1983 struck hardest at two distinct groups of countries. At one extreme, they included a handful of Eastern European and advanced developing countries heavily dependent on international market finance. At the other, they included some small, very poor countries, almost wholly dependent on raw material exports, whose prices fell steeply, and official foreign aid, whose levels stagnated. Out of 154 borrowing countries statistically covered by the Bank for International Settlements, 35 interrupted external debt service during the two years through mid-1984, but 119 continued to service their foreign obligations in full (Table 2, page 60).

2 • A longer perspective

Present events and options for the future are thrown into sharper relief when set in a longer perspective. The progression to the world's present difficulties has not been sudden by any means. It is now twenty years since those difficulties began to emerge, more than ten years since they became universally apparent, and five years since they became acute. The process has been marked throughout by periods of timid official policy followed by frightened and belated overreaction. It began with a long, dilatory, and inconclusive quest for a reform of the Bretton Woods monetary system, which ended with its sudden and total abandonment in 1971. A gradual twenty-year slide in real world oil prices was followed by an abrupt and crippling increase in 1973 and another rise in 1979. A concerted boom engineered by the main financial powers in the early 1970s produced an inflationary explosion and was succeeded by a sharp but very brief recession in 1974–75. The failure to adjust to higher real fuel prices led to the brutal monetary disinflation that began in 1979 and from which an uncertain recovery has only recently started.

The destructively wide fluctuations of the world business cycle and of exchange and interest rates during the past fifteen years have merely reflected violent swings in official policies between the fumbling of "gradualism" and the recklessness of dramatic "solutions." However, important continuities persist beneath the surface. The ways in which countries settle their international payments with each other change periodically. So do the ways by which the development process takes place. But although the mechanics change, the essentials remain basically the same.

The international balance of payments is one constant factor in the equation. The current account of any country's balance of payments with the rest of the world consists of net earnings on trade in goods, plus investment income, plus net "invisible" earnings from services like shipping, insurance, and tourism provided to nonresidents and paid for in foreign currency. Countries in current surplus are net exporters of capital, and those in current deficit are net importers of capital. A current surplus is always exactly matched by a rise in national reserves of foreign currencies, which can be spent on purchases abroad, or by an export of capital, or by some combination of the two. To the extent that a current deficit cannot be financed by drawing down reserves, it has to be financed by imports of capital, meaning international borrowing and the attraction of investment from abroad.

In the latter part of the nineteenth century and the earlier part of the twentieth, payments between countries were adjusted in an apparently invisible fashion, as they still are within countries today. That happened because only one form of money was used internationally, just as one form of money is still used within the borders of any sovereign state. During the forty years of the full international gold standard, which prevailed until 1914, international payments seemed to adjust automatically. Any country that spent more than it earned immediately suffered a drain of gold to countries that earned more than they spent. Deficit countries were then forced to adjust by some combination of importing less or exporting more. In theory, that system of automatic adjustment was sharp and even brutal, but in practice, it was often softened by loans of gold from one country to another.

It is a romantic illusion, however, to think of the gold standard as one that had endured for centuries. On the contrary, before that system began its brief international reign from the late nineteenth century until World War I, gold, silver, and other commodities competed with one another for supremacy as means of payment. The states of medieval Germany had about 600 currencies, and every Italian city had its own. Active foreign exchange and arbitrage markets enlivened the trade fairs of medieval and Renaissance Europe.

The international gold standard was abruptly abandoned with the onset of World War I. An attempt was made to return to the international use of gold through a modified gold standard after the war. In 1922, at a conference in Genoa, the major financial powers agreed to "economise in the monetary use of gold." Under that agreement, only a few currencies were backed directly by gold, and other countries used those "key" currencies as their reserves. Since the United States was the only major country still on the gold standard, the dollar became the international "key" currency. However, Britain and some European countries returned to a modified gold bullion standard from 1925 to 1931. Sterling then served as a second major currency that could be used by countries to make international payments and in which they could hold their reserves.*

But a growing divergence of national economic policies created ever

*Under the gold standard, bank notes were fully backed by gold. Under the gold bullion standard, convertibility was provided only into standard bars of 400 troy ounces, meaning that it was available only to institutions and rich individuals.

larger imbalances in international payments, and countries were unwilling to correct those imbalances in the prompt and harsh fashion required by the automatic operation of even the modified gold bullion standard. That system consequently broke down and was followed by a period of competitive devaluations, import and foreign exchange controls, and other devices intended to shield countries from the harsh realities of a world recession. Yet the supposedly protective measures that proliferated made the world's recession even worse.

The Genoa agreement of 1922 to conserve gold by the use of some "key" currencies did, however, provide one of the elements of the Bretton Woods monetary system created in 1944. In practice, although it was not laid down in the rules, the system came to be based on limited convertibility of gold through the dollar alone. The American authorities agreed to exchange dollars for gold at a fixed price of $35 an ounce to foreign official dollar-holders in balance-of-payments need. That undertaking by the United States underpinned the fixed exchange rates of the Bretton Woods system. The distinguishing feature of Bretton Woods was that it represented the first attempt in history at a treaty monetary system, with the International Monetary Fund as its monitor. Countries that joined the IMF signed an international agreement that bound them to its rules. Those rules required member countries to maintain the exchange rates of their currencies except in the undefined extremity of a "fundamental disequilibrium" in their international payments. Any threat to the exchange rate therefore gave a strong and highly visible signal of the need for adjustment by countries whose currencies became subject to pressure on the exchanges.

In practice, however, it was only the major industrial countries that were subjected to this particular discipline because the staff of the IMF regularly encouraged devaluation as a means of adjustment for developing countries. Moreover, even among the industrial countries, adjustment was asymmetrical. Deficit countries adjusted their economies to avoid devaluation and were given conditional financing by the IMF to provide time for an orderly improvement of their external balances of payments. Surplus countries, however, were rarely subject to similar pressures to upvalue their currencies, although the rules of the IMF had envisaged economic adjustment and, in the last resort, exchange rate changes for surplus and deficit countries alike. That asymmetry was one reason why the Bretton Woods fixed exchange rate system broke down in 1971. Another was growing external pressure on the dollar, the currency on which the whole system rested. But at root, the causes of breakdown were a growing divergence of national economic policies, increasing differentials between national inflation rates, and growing imbalances of international payments, whose consequences national governments were unwilling to face until overwhelmed by events.

Attempts to reform the treaty monetary system were not formally abandoned until the beginning of 1974. But since 1971, the world has lived with fluctuating exchange rates, as it has through most of history. Money is created by national central banks and is moved around the world by official agencies and commercial banks, but at rates of exchange that alter constantly to reflect the balance of supply and demand.

Floating exchange rates supposedly give national governments greater independence in managing their economies. But experience since 1971 has simply driven home the point that floating exchange rates are merely another self-adjusting mechanism. An unchecked fall in a country's exchange rate increases the price of imports in terms of domestic currency and so has inflationary consequences that ultimately lead to an adjustment in domestic economic policy. On the other hand, an unchecked rise in a country's exchange rate erodes the competitiveness of its products in domestic and international markets, likewise forcing, in time, a change of domestic economic policy.

It is impossible to know whether the international gold standard of the forty years to 1914 and the system of orderly exchange rates, which prevailed for just over twenty years to 1971, contributed to the world economy's relative stability during those two periods. The two systems may have merely reflected underlying stability. But the indisputable fact is that countries have never been able to live beyond their means under any form of monetary system without at some point being forced to adjust to the realities of the world. Admittedly, there have always been some exceptions. In today's world, Israel and some small Central American countries are subsidized by the United States for strategic and political reasons, just as Elizabeth I of England subsidized the Dutch in the fight against Spain four centuries ago. But such exceptions merely prove the rule. And, if present debt difficulties have any lessons, reading the different kind of signals given by floating exchange rates is one of them.

3 • The development process

To say that countries cannot indefinitely live beyond their means by spending more than they earn is different from saying that all countries should aim for exact balance or surpluses in their current transactions with the rest of the world. Indeed, it is literally impossible for all countries to earn current surpluses at the same time. It is normal and desirable for developing countries to run current deficits, provided the offsetting capital inflows are invested, along with domestic savings, in ways that increase net foreign exchange earnings over time. That development process is obviously in the interests of both capital-importing and capital-exporting countries, albeit in different ways. New and profitable investment opportunities are created for the excess savings of capital-exporting countries; and the growing prosperity of the recipients increases the world market for trade in goods and services, increasing the prosperity of all.

With the rare exceptions of countries obtaining large "windfall" gains from their possession of easily and cheaply exploitable scarce natural resources, like Saudi Arabia's oil, all countries go through long periods in which they must augment their domestic savings with borrowed foreign resources to finance their economic development. That process continues until a country has reached a stage of prosperity at which domestic savings exceed the opportunities for further profitable investment at home, leaving a surplus for more rewarding investment abroad. At that point, countries join the ranks of net capital exporters.

The process is not new. Throughout the nineteenth century, Europe exported capital to the "new" worlds, particularly to America and Australasia. Such capital was used mainly to finance infrastructure, especially transportation systems, to provide a foundation for further economic growth in the capital-importing countries. The United States did not become a net capital exporter until the turn of the century, a transition made later still by some of today's richest countries, such as Switzerland.*

*The fact that rich countries tend to run chronic current surpluses as net capital exporters is not contradicted by their periodic lapse into cyclical deficits. The United States ran such deficits in 1971–72, in 1977–79, and again from 1982. Each time in the past, a dollar "crisis" enforced a return to current surpluses, and at some point America's current payments will doubtless move back to surplus once again.

Another illustration of the role of international capital in the development process is provided by the lending record of the World Bank, which initially supplied capital for the reconstruction of Europe and Japan after World War II. The Bank then went on to make loans to a succession of countries, which eventually "graduated" from the Bank to the market. Other countries that used to obtain concessional financing from the Bank's "soft loan" affiliate, the International Development Association, subsequently "graduated" to borrowing on the harder, more market-related terms of the Bank itself. A few of those countries then moved another step forward, gaining acceptance as borrowers in the financial markets.

Such a progression provides evidence of the historical links between international debt and development and also illustrates the continuity of the development process. The participants are not frozen in a tableau; on the contrary, their roles are changed by the very act of their participation.

Another constant of the development process is the subtle interplay between creditor and debtor countries, which determines the size and persistence of current deficits and the volume of offsetting capital flows. It is increasingly difficult to trace the flows statistically, but it is axiomatic that the world's balance of payments must balance. The sum of net surpluses earned on current transactions by any set of countries will always be exactly matched by the net combined deficits incurred by the rest of the world's countries.

The ability and willingness of deficit countries to run up external debt help determine the surpluses that other countries can run in combination. Potential or actual constraints on the debt-servicing capacities of deficit countries limit the surpluses that creditor countries can earn. That interplay, which can reinforce a stagnation or actual contraction of world trade, was graphically illustrated during the three-year global disinflation that began in 1979. The value of world trade contracted from 1980 to 1983, even in terms of an appreciating dollar. The volume of world trade therefore shrank still more, and even the oil exporters' cartel weakened in the face of declining world demand.

How capital moves across frontiers

The international economic development process, like the world's payment systems within which it takes place, is marked by an underlying constancy. But there have been some important changes over time in the ways by which capital is moved around the world.

Until the end of World War II, there were three predominant channels by which capital flowed across frontiers. One of them was foreign direct investment, consisting of the establishment or purchase of a business, or the controlling share of a business, in one country by a company headquartered in another country. This was a particularly important form of foreign investment for American corporations in the early years of the twentieth century, when antitrust legislation in the United States helped prompt American companies to look abroad for opportunities denied them at home. Foreign direct investment once more became important for American corporations during the decade following 1945, when foreign countries lacked dollars to import American goods. More recently, a worldwide proliferation of nontariff barriers to trade has given fresh impetus to foreign direct investment by international companies in the mature and newer industrialized countries as an alternative to the export of goods and services.

A second traditional channel for international capital flows was provided by foreign portfolio investment, consisting of the purchase by the residents of one country of securities issued by the governments of other countries, or the purchase of shares in foreign companies by nonresidents.*

A third historic channel for international capital flows consisted of "traditional" or "classical" foreign bonds. These are sold for nonresident borrowers in the domestic bond markets of another country, for instance bonds sold for Canadian borrowers in New York or for Austrian borrowers in Zurich. The issue of such bonds on a regular basis, first in Amsterdam and thereafter in London, goes back more than two centuries. Up to the early twentieth century, such international issues made on behalf of governments and private companies carried very high risk premiums. It was common for investment bankers who marketed such bonds to support the prices of those bonds during periods of adversity, as Nathan Mayer Rothschild supported French government bonds on the London market during the French invasion of Spain in 1823. The legendary financier was acting exactly as commercial banks act today when they tide over borrowers in difficulties. International bondholders often lost their money through repudiation or default, and it is only in the past generation that bondholders have come to assume that their interests will be specially protected, like those of small depositors in the banking system.

The role of official policy

Savings continue to flow from surplus to deficit countries through the three channels described above. However, after World War II, govern-

*Since 1982 the United States has run record current deficits financed by international portfolio investment from abroad. The world has, in effect, helped finance America's growing budget deficits.

ments played an increasing role individually and through international agencies such as the International Monetary Fund and the World Bank.

From 1945 until about 1965, the movement of capital across the world became, to a very large extent, an act of official foreign and economic policy. Western governments and international agencies transferred resources for the reconstruction of Europe and Japan after World War II, and then for the development of poorer countries. The United States, which started this process, wanted political control over capital transfers through the Marshall Plan and also in its subsequent bilateral aid. When other Western countries became aid donors, they were similarly motivated.

Recently, development aid has been provided by governments of the richer oil-exporting countries and the governments of some of the newer industrialized countries as well as by the governments of Western industrialized countries. Development aid, a term used to describe all official capital flows, consists of grants (meaning gifts), concessional aid in the form of loans made at rates of interest below market rates, and export credits similarly provided at less than market rates, mostly to finance sales of plant and equipment to foreign, including developing, countries.*

Official aid flows have been considered desirable partly on humanitarian grounds. More prosaically, however, aid has been sold to the legislatures of donor countries as an instrument of foreign policy, and to Western industry and trade unions as a subsidy for exports and jobs. Much bilateral aid is "tied" to the purchase of goods and services by the recipient country from the donor country.

Private international capital flows were stimulated during the early 1960s on an unprecedented scale as the unintended result of official policies, above all those of the United States. The United States introduced a set of regulations in 1963 intended to stem the flow of dollars abroad and so win time for an orderly reform of the Bretton Woods system. The regulations included constraints limiting the access of many foreign borrowers to the U.S. bond market. In addition, they required U.S. companies to finance their foreign investments abroad. Moreover, they came into being at a time when the interest rates that U.S. banks were allowed to pay on large time deposits were still restricted.

The new capital export controls did not reduce the flow of dollars

---

*Military aid, although often large, is not dealt with in this report, partly because much of it goes unrecorded. However, money being fungible, aid provided for one purpose can release resources in the recipient country for alternative deployment.

abroad. Coupled with the existing banking restrictions, the regulations simply encouraged the export abroad of a large part of the American money and capital markets, where they have remained ever since. Throughout the 1960s, U.S. banks rushed to open branches in London and other foreign centers. American corporations placed their idle dollar balances with U.S. and other banks outside the United States at rates of deposit dictated by the markets alone. And American and other international corporations also borrowed dollars from American and other banks outside the United States that were free of official restraint, to finance their international trade and investment.

The American measures of the early 1960s, coupled with measures by the German, Swiss, and Dutch authorities to limit international flows into Deutschemark, Swiss francs, and guilders, all gave a considerable stimulus to the growth of new international money and capital markets that had begun during the previous decade. In the late 1970s, international bank lending increased very rapidly, reaching $1.4 trillion outstanding by 1983 (Table 3, page 62). However, such lending began to slow down in 1982 and 1983 (see Tables 4 and 5, pages 63 and 64).

4 • Eurocurrencies and Eurocredits

The international money market, which usually provides funds for up to a year, is the base on which a large part of the international capital market functions.

The main international money market is the Eurocurrencies market, where currencies are lent and borrowed, as distinct from the foreign exchanges, where they are bought and sold. But the two markets are joined in numerous ways; the participants in them are almost exclusively banks (plus a few multinational companies), and their business is conducted by telephone around the world and around the clock.

A Eurocurrency is simply a foreign currency for at least one of the banks in a lending transaction, and often for both. For instance, a dollar deposited in New York is simply a dollar. The same dollar deposited with a bank outside the United States, including at a U.S. bank abroad, is a Eurodollar. The same holds true for externally placed sterling, Swiss francs, Deutschemarks, yen, or any other currency, which then becomes Eurosterling, Euro-Swiss francs, and so on.

When a bank in London lends dollars to a bank in Amsterdam, the London bank has acquired a foreign currency, or a Eurodollar claim, and the Dutch bank has run up a Eurodollar liability. However, ultimate settlement can be made only in the currency's country of origin. Correspondent banks in New York debit the account of the London bank and credit that of the Amsterdam bank.

Although banks in the Euromarket are supervised, especially the large ones that dominate it, the market itself is free from regulation, which gives it an unrivaled efficiency.

The short-term Eurocurrencies market provides international banks with a large part of the funds that they transform into medium- and occasionally longer-term loans to governments, government agencies, and private sector borrowers, predominantly large companies, in both the industrialized and developing worlds. Thus reference to a country's foreign debt is shorthand for the external debt of its government, official agencies, and private borrowers combined.

Medium-term international bank loans, known as Eurocredits, are mostly made by syndicates of banks, meaning banks that combine to provide a particular loan, rather than permanent groupings of banks. That system derives from American practice. Because of the fragmentation of the U.S. banking system, it is common for American corporations to have several bankers and common, also, for regional banks to invite the participation of larger money center banks when they arrange loans for their own customers.

In the international market, nearly all medium-term bank loans are provided at prearranged margins above the cost of money to the lending banks, the total cost to the borrower being adjusted every three or six months. For example, if the underlying interbank three-months' dollar deposit rate is 9 percent, and the agreed lending margin 1 percent, the borrower pays 10 percent. If, after three months, the interbank rate falls to 8 percent, the borrower pays 9 percent for the ensuing period, and so on.

The Eurocurrencies and Eurocredits markets were already well established when the first "oil shock" of 1973 created a sudden and massive shift of savings from oil-importing to oil-exporting countries. The markets rapidly filled a gap that governments and international agencies, such as the International Monetary Fund and World Bank, did not. Although most of the capital channeled through the international bank loan and bond markets went to industrialized countries, a considerable volume went to a handful of advanced developing countries and newer industrialized countries, particularly in Latin America and Southeast Asia.

During 1981, the year before the present international debt difficulties surfaced, 67 percent of new Eurocredits went to mature industrialized countries, 28 percent to non-oil-developing countries (LDCs), 4 percent to members of OPEC, and 1 percent to Eastern Europe (Table 5). Eurocredit lending to non-oil LDCs continued to be as highly concentrated as it had been for the preceding dozen years. In 1981, more than half of all new Eurocredits going to non-OPEC LDCs were provided to borrowers in Mexico and Brazil, and those countries and four others (Argentina, Chile, South Korea, and Malaysia) together received about 90 percent of the total.

While medium-term borrowing from commercial banks offers considerable advantages, it also entails risks. During the three-year global disinflation, which began in 1979, the risks suddenly became acute. The cost of new and outstanding debt to all borrowers increased steeply, and at the same time, their opportunities for earning the money needed to service debt were severely constrained.

The advantages of the Eurocredits market for borrowers include the quick availability of capital in larger amounts than in the international fixed-interest bond markets. Eurocredits also usually involve fewer formalities and, before debt-servicing difficulties arose, fewer conditions about their use than funds from international agencies and other official donors. Apart from providing capital on a scale not obtainable from official donors in the 1970s, the Eurocredits markets also filled well-known "gaps" in official aid by providing more generalized balance-of-payments financing, financing of the total and not just the foreign exchange cost of development investments, and financing the recurrent and not merely initial foreign exchange costs of such investments.

The lack of conditionality about use gave borrowing countries considerable flexibility in the deployment of such market funds, allowing them to build up reserves at times of favorable borrowing conditions. At the same time, a good record in the Eurocredits markets allowed developing countries such as Brazil, Mexico, and Singapore, as well as an East European country such as Hungary, to borrow in international bond markets. The amounts raised in international bond markets by such borrowers were relatively small, but acceptance as borrowers in the bond markets further increased their credit standing, allowing them to borrow at even better terms in the larger Eurocredits markets.

A drawback for international Eurocredit borrowers is that such market funds are more expensive than official capital and thus drive up the total cost of a fixed element in the balance of payments. More important is the floating and unpredictable cost of Eurocredit borrowing. The three-months' Eurodollar base rate, to which most floating rate Eurocredit lending is tied, rose from less than 9 percent to about 20 percent between 1978 and 1981, fell back to 9 percent in 1983, and then rose again to 12 percent by mid-1984. According to the Bank for International Settlements, each one-point change in dollar interest rates had an impact of $1.4 billion on the combined annualized debt service of Argentina, Brazil, Mexico, and Venezuela by 1983.

5 • The role of governments in the debt buildup

According to the conspiracy theory of recent history, the governments of Western industrialized countries put pressure on their commercial banks to step up their international lending to friendly countries during the debt buildup of the 1970s. There is little evidence to support this view, however, and a wealth of evidence that banks simply acted, as borrowing countries did, in response to perceived needs and opportunities. Western governments and their agencies did exercise varying degrees of persuasion in particular instances, but there is no basis for the belief that systematic pressure existed or that occasional suasion played more than a marginal role.

The promotion of trade has become an ever more important aspect of the foreign policy of most countries, industrialized and developing alike. Arms sales, falling into a category of their own, are directly promoted between governments, and after the oil price increase of 1973 some oil-exporting countries purchased huge amounts at steeply rising prices; of course, the arms-producing countries were happy to sell them in order to help pay their enlarged oil import bills. Arnon Gafny, then governor of Israel's central bank, estimated in 1979 that the value of arms sales to the Middle East had risen from $1.5 billion to more than $20 billion a year between 1966 and 1977.*

Governments try to promote their exports by a variety of means. For example, helping their companies obtain foreign supply contracts is a routine function of Western and other embassies. In addition, banks usually finance the exports of their corporate clients or provide finance to help the foreign counterpart make the purchase. There is also competition between the governments of Western industrialized countries, as well as the governments of some newer industrialized countries, to promote exports. Governments often provide subsidized medium-term credits to facilitate exports of capital goods by their own nations' corporations, a form of "trade war" that twenty-two industrialized countries have been trying to contain within the forum of the Organization for Economic Cooperation and Development since 1974.

---

*"Israel: A Treaty without Peace," *The Banker,* London, May 1979.

However, all such official encouragement of international lending has been marginal in relation to the global climate created by the often conflicting or, even worse, coincidental domestic economic demand management policies of the major financial powers. For example, the result of the efforts of the leading financial powers to restore business confidence after the presumed shock of the Bretton Woods breakdown in 1971 produced an inflationary boom in 1972–73 that was greater than intended by any single government. It contributed to a belated and very large increase in world energy prices, which had the deflationary effect of a sales tax imposed on oil users by oil producers. Ownership of a large part of world savings changed hands, but the savings remained in the international commercial banking system and were used to help finance the current payments deficits of oil-importing countries in the industrialized and developing worlds. The market filled a vacuum after governments and international agencies failed to move more funds following the growing imbalance in international current payments during the 1970s.

Aside from Japan, Switzerland, and some Southeast Asian economies, most countries made only a brief and partial adjustment to higher fuel prices by reducing their spending, increasing their foreign earnings, or some combination of the two. After a brief recession in 1974–75, most countries tried to spend their way out of their difficulties. By the beginning of 1980, consumer price inflation in the OECD countries had again risen to its 1974 peak of 14 percent, from a previous low of just under 8 percent at the end of 1977 (and about 4 percent in the 1960s).

Renewed inflation contributed to a second rise in world oil prices at the end of 1979, restoring them in real terms to their approximate 1974 level. Even before that happened, Paul Volcker, the chairman of the U.S. Federal Reserve Board, mounted a sudden and determined counterinflationary policy in the midst of a dollar crisis. The Federal Reserve switched in October 1979 from a policy of trying to manage the money supply through price (by influencing interest rates) to a more direct monetarist approach. The actual volume of credit was strictly controlled through regulations requiring U.S. banks to set aside a larger proportion of their deposit liabilities in the form of required reserves held as vault cash or deposited with the Federal Reserve System.

The U.S. monetary disinflation, quickly followed by all other major financial powers, rapidly brought about a global recession from which the world began an uncertain recovery only in the second half of 1982. By that time, average OECD consumer price inflation had been brought down to about 5 percent, and then stabilized at that level in 1983 and 1984.

Those violent policy changes created the conditions that led advanced developing countries and newer industrialized countries to borrow heavily on world capital markets to finance enlarged current payments deficits and build up reserves on favorable terms. International banks competed keenly to enter international lending on a new scale, partly because of insufficient loan demand in their home countries and partly because of the profitability of the wholesale international lending business. The big banks constantly complained in the 1970s about narrow lending spreads in what they called a "borrowers' market," but they continued to compete for international lending because the returns to banks were not as low as suggested by actual lending margins (Table 6, page 64).

The average cost of funds, especially dollars, has always been lower for large banks, particularly banks with a U.S. retail deposit base, than Libor, the London interbank offered rate for dollar deposits, which serves as a standard benchmark over which lending spreads are fixed. In addition, banks receive fees from borrowers for arranging or managing syndicated loans, as well as fees for keeping funds ready until actually drawn by borrowers (standby fees). Although management fees are shared, the largest shares go to the biggest banks managing the credits, which are also those banks obtaining their funds at the lowest average cost.

While the economic demand management policies of leading Western governments created the climate and the conditions for an enlarged flow of commercial bank lending to developing countries, the stance of Western governments ensured a financing vacuum that only the banking system could fill. This can be considered either an act of policy or as policy by default, but as a matter of fact, governments did not fill the vacuum.

A striking characteristic of the 1960s and 1970s was the gap at each stage between official paralysis and private initiative. The 1960s were taken up by "urgent" international negotiations to create more international liquidity through the issue of special drawing rights on the International Monetary Fund. The net result was the creation of about $10 billion of SDRs between 1970 and 1972 and another $15 billion from 1978 to 1981, for a total now equaling about 6 percent of official world reserves and less than 0.5 percent of world liquidity as represented by the international assets of the world's commercial banking system. Meanwhile, the size of the Eurocurrencies market, as estimated by the Bank for International Settlements, rose about tenfold to $60 billion in the 1960s and then grew ten times once again in the 1970s, to an estimated $600 billion net by the end of that decade. Its net size now is about $1 trillion.

Another example of the difference between official inaction and market achievement was the contrast between the "urgent" attempts by the International Monetary Fund to mobilize a special oil-financing facility and the size of the loans made by international banks. The IMF produced a grand total of $7 billion; international bank lending was running at an average of $125 billion a year during the last three years of the 1970s with nearly $25 billion a year net going to non-oil-developing countries during that time, according to the 1983 IMF annual report.

Third, there was the initiative taken in 1974 by Henry Kissinger, as secretary of state, to assemble a "safety net" from the member countries of the OECD that would provide government guarantees for up to $24 billion of commerical bank recycling. After long negotiation, this was approved by the legislatures of all the OECD member countries, with the embarrassing exception of the U.S. Congress, whose refusal put an end to the scheme.

Experience has shown that any international initative requiring the agreement of legislatures, especially that of the uniquely independent U.S. Congress, is unlikely to produce quick and large results. That may be welcomed or regretted, but is best accepted as a fact. On the other hand, action not needing legislative approval has sometimes been taken quickly, as in the case of the Herstatt banking crisis of 1974 and the Mexican debt moratorium of 1982 (both of which will be discussed later).

6 • Where interests conflict and coincide

Almost a generation of unprecedented economic recovery and growth in the older Western industrial countries came to an end after the sudden inflationary boom of 1972–73, and since then those economies have expanded by fits and starts. The change, which was marked rather than caused by the sudden rise of world fuel prices, coincided with the emergence of a structural change in the global economy. More developing countries were becoming competitors in world export markets for capital goods and consumer goods, whose output was formerly a near monopoly of the older Western economies. It is difficult, however, to make any precise connection between waning growth in the older industrialized economies and the emergence of new competitors, except to observe that the two phenomena coincided and reinforced the problems faced by governments, industry, labor, and the financial markets.

In the older Western economies, the warning signs became more noticeable after 1974. They included a flattening or decline in the share of profits in national income in most Western countries and a similar weakening of fixed capital expenditures, that is, investment in new plant and equipment. Considerable excess capacity, resulting partly from earlier, synchronized investment booms, emerged and still persists in certain industries, notably steel, shipbuilding, textiles, synthetic fibers, and some petroleum chemical industries.

The coincidence of slower or more fitful growth in the mature Western economies and an apparent change in the structure of the global economy intensified conflicts between social and economic groups within countries. It led also to sharper conflicts between countries, which found its expression partly in a proliferation of nontariff barriers to international trade.

The difficulties of the present transition, in which some countries and industries face new competition as others seize new opportunities, cannot be denied. Japan, which led the way in providing new competition to the established economic powers of North America and Europe, has been challenged in its turn by growing competition in regional and world markets from countries such as Korea, Singapore, Taiwan, the Philippines, Brazil, Mexico, Yugoslavia, and the British crown colony of Hong

Kong. This development is not accidental, but rather the result of a consistent Western policy since 1945, based on the belief that growing prosperity in more countries will ultimately help to enrich all. The difficulties of a relatively prolonged transition may not have been fully realized, but once started, the pace of such progressions cannot be controlled, even when the eventual outcome continues to be regarded as the desirable one of a richer world.

The international capital markets performed a major role in balancing payments between countries. Thus banks were thrust into a policy role because their large-scale international lending involved them, at least passively, in determining priorities for capital-importing countries. Moreover, such political influence, exercised passively in the act of providing finance, was exercised less passively when the banking system temporarily shut out of the market some countries that had overborrowed, such as Italy in 1974 and Britain in 1976. Such forms of influence are exercised more openly, even if through the agency of the International Monetary Fund, when economic adjustment is enforced on countries that have interrupted full service of their foreign debt.

When governments left a greatly increased share of international financing to the banking system in the 1970s, and when commercial banks accepted the function assigned to them by default, each side became hostage to the other. Banks put some of their independence at risk, while governments abandoned some of the control they had formerly exercised through their direction of international financial flows.

To the extent that governments provide international capital, it is a reasonable presumption that the donor governments have considered and are willing to face the eventual consequences for their electorates of helping to bring new foreign trade competitors into being. When international capital transfers take the form of foreign direct investment, it is reasonable to presume that international companies with specialized knowledge of trends in their fields of operation will concentrate new investment where it will fit with existing investment elsewhere.

On the other hand, market capital flowing to borrowing countries through the commercial banking system is not similarly controlled. Market capital provided to borrowers outside the mature industrialized world tends to go in a highly concentrated way to a handful of newly industrialized and economically advanced developing countries. Despite much talk by bankers of project financing, very little international bank financing is tied, in the way that much official aid is tied, to purchases by the recipient from the donor country. Unlike foreign direct investment, which is concentrated heavily on the exploitation of natural resources in developing countries, bank financing makes a wider contribution directly and indirectly to industrial development in the recipient countries. Allowing for mistakes and waste at the margin, international market financing has tended to be more efficient than official aid or foreign direct investment. But, to the extent that it has been more efficient, it has also helped speed the process by which mature industrialized countries are faced with new competition from advanced developing countries both in the quest for raw materials and for export markets.

In essence, flexible and resilient financial markets fulfilled their proper role of helping industrialized and developing countries to adapt to economic shocks and growing changes in the structure of the global economy during the 1970s. In the words first applied to its own lending by the International Monetary Fund many years ago, they provided and at present continue to provide "time, but not time to waste." However, that time horizon is now shrinking. In the last resort, financial markets cannot and do not allow countries to avoid the costs of real adjustment indefinitely.

The conflicts brought to a head in the present situation are difficult precisely because they do not involve disembodied protagonists. Debt is deferred trade. Western banks depend on an expansion of Western markets to allow borrowing countries to earn the export income they need to service their foreign debt. Yet more industries in the mature industrial countries and more workers in those industries have come to see their survival in terms of protection from "unfair" foreign competition.

Although the interests of those involved conflict in some ways, in others they are closely entwined. Borrowing countries, which find severe retrenchment politically difficult, nevertheless have a strong self-interest in a return to full debt service and good credit standing. Western banks, which would like to see debtor countries return to full debt service, nevertheless have an interest in their domestic corporate customers, including companies vulnerable to foreign competition.

The governments of the mature industrialized countries, concerned about the highest rates of unemployment experienced since the depression of the 1930s, are nevertheless critically dependent on the maintenance of a stable financial system and sustained, uninflationary economic growth—and that cannot be achieved in the absence of an open world trading system. At root, the conflict between the special and general interest exists even within the individual. The automobile worker in Detroit or Coventry has a general interest in a free trading system that will give him the choice of the best goods, wherever produced, at the lowest prices. But he may see his special interest, correctly, in the preservation of his job, which carries with it his very way of life and the surroundings in which he lives it.

The complexity of conflicts of interest within the participants rather than only between them has contributed to the present international debt impasse; the resolution of these conflicts, while admittedly very difficult to achieve, is critical.

The precedent of the 1930s

The only precedent for the present international debt impasse was the suspension of foreign debt service in the 1930s by Germany, Austria, and some East European and Latin American countries. Those events provide some useful financial and political analogies with the present.

As already mentioned, the amount of international debt restructured after 1931 totaled more than $80 billion in present value. By far the biggest single amount was owed by Germany, and Germany's moratorium had its origins in the hyperinflation of 1922–23, which was the result of the decision by the Kaiser's government not to increase taxes, but to fight the war of 1914–18 entirely on credit. Karl Helfferich, the secretary of state, explained official policy in 1916 when he assured German investors in Hindenburg war bonds that the full cost of the war would be debited to the enemy. When the outcome made that impracticable, the Weimar government found itself with no alternative but to wipe out the debt to German investors, which it had inherited, and it did so by debasing the currency. That done, the Reichsmark stabilized of its own accord.*

The Weimar government's hyperinflationary policy also wiped out the debt of German business and industry, which was able to start life again with a clean slate. What remained of the savings of the German middle class disappeared in the deluge, but foreign funds flooded into Germany from 1924 until a withdrawal began following the Wall Street crash of 1929. Those withdrawals reached panic proportions after the collapse of Austria's Creditanstalt in June 1931, and in the following month the collapse of Germany's Darmstadter und Nazional Bank led instantly to the declaration of a banking moratorium and tight foreign exchange controls in Germany. Such, briefly, were the events that led to the renegotiation of terms covering the modern equivalent of about $75 billion, owed to foreign private and public creditors by private and public debtors in Germany, Austria, and some East European countries.

---

*Hjalmar Schacht, the Brooklyn-born president of the Reichsbank, was engagingly frank about these events in his memoirs, written in the 1960s. He claimed none of the "wizardry" attributed to him for restabilizing the Reichsmark. Instead, he recalled the promise that the 1914 war would cost the German people nothing and added, acidly, "Churchill was more honest in 1940 when he promised the British people nothing but blood, sweat, toil and tears."

Nearly 90 percent of that debt was owed by Germany, and within days a credit for the modern equivalent of about $17 billion was provided to the Reichsbank by the Bank of England, the Banque de France, and the New York Federal Reserve Bank. At the same time, commercial banking creditors met in London under the chairmanship of an American banker and agreed, as a first step, to prolong all outstanding cash advances to Germany for six months and to renew automatically or replace maturing German acceptance credits. Those quick actions were similar to current efforts to persuade Western banks to maintain or even increase credit lines to the banks of troubled debtor countries in the Eurocurrencies interbank market. The object, then as now, was to ensure that the debtor country could go on trading internationally in order to earn its way back to full debt service and credit standing. The German debt standstill of 1931 was extended several times.

As in some present debt renegotiations, payments due to Germany's foreign creditors on outstanding debt as well as on some exports to Germany were effectively blocked in "registered" Reichsmark accounts at the German central bank. The foreign creditors could invest those "registered" Reichsmark in German bonds, use them for "additional" imports from Germany, or discount them abroad.

Many foreign creditors cut some of their losses by discounting "registered" Reichsmark abroad to purchasers willing to take on "additional" German goods, but at the cost of depressing output and jobs in those countries receiving "dumped" imports from Germany. An overvalued Reichsmark shielded by exchange controls held down the domestic currency cost to German industry of imports. And Germany was able to rebuild its exports, which were paid for at less than the official exchange rate in terms of discounted "registered" Reichsmark. In effect, Germany was permitted to run a dual exchange rate by creditors who settled for part of a loaf rather than none.

Economic recovery and the rearmament of the 1930s helped revive world trade. The French government accepted settlement of its claims mainly in the form of coal deliveries in 1939; debt to Switzerland was cleared early in World War II to ensure the availability of highly specialized strategic imports from Switzerland during the war; and the debt to the United States and Britain was cleared, finally, in the 1950s.*

The Latin American countries, which had suspended service on about $5 billion in the 1930s, also refrained from formally repudiating

*Paul Bareau, "The Lessons of the Earlier International Debt Crisis," *The Banker*, London, December 1983.

their external debts and eventually repaid part of those debts in the 1940s and 1950s to pave their reentry into the world markets as borrowers.*

Then as now, the developing countries of Eastern Europe and Latin America were overwhelmed by a world recession that turned domestic policy shortcomings into a crisis. So was Germany, although its difficulties originated in the decision to fight the war of 1914–18 by borrowing from its citizens, rather than taxing them. The squandering of a generation's savings left Germany excessively dependent on foreign capital, which flooded in and then out. Yet the German experience merely represented in an extreme form the root of debt difficulties wherever and whenever encountered, which consists of willing the end without the means.

The prompt rescue mounted by the authorities of Germany's main creditor countries was very similar to the reaction of the monetary authorities after 1982, but the discounting of "registered" Reichsmark, with its indirect support for employment in Germany at the cost of employment elsewhere, has not been repeated this time. The nearest modern equivalent has been the resale of international loan participations by some banks to others, but this has not had a depressing effect on the world economy.

A major difference is that most international debt in the 1930s consisted of bonds, and it took more than a generation to restore the confidence of investors in foreign bond issues. Being less powerful than banks, bondholders fared worse, and, in the case of developing countries, they have never again provided a major source of imported capital. Developing countries had to wait for the large-scale international bank loan market to emerge from the late 1960s. Bondholders have acquired special treatment by demanding and getting exceptional respect from borrowers; as a result, developing countries have come to borrow on international bond markets for the sake of prestige and enhanced credit ratings, rather than for the relatively small sums available to them there. The closest modern equivalent of the international bondholders of the 1930s are the world's smaller banks, which have tended to withdraw from international lending except for self-liquidating short-term trade finance provided to fund the exports of their own customers. They, too, may come to exact special terms of some kind as the price of their eventual reentry into the international lending market, and, although their role in that market is marginal, margins are nevertheless critical.

A different set of questions is posed by the political impact of Germany's 1922–23 hyperinflation and rising unemployment from the late

*Anatole Kaletsky, "When the Debtors Said No," *Financial Times* (London), December 28, 1983.

1920s. In wiping out the savings of a generation, hyperinflation unquestionably traumatized a people conditioned to venerate industry and thrift. That experience, followed by depression and unemployment, doubtless contributed to the growing popularity of the Nazis. However, although world depression similarly spawned extremist parties in the democracies in the 1930s, they remained on the fringes. While Germany's economic disorder may help explain the appeal of the Nazis, it does not explain their ability to seize power. The special factor in Germany was that the collapse of the Hohenzollern monarchy in 1918 left a power vacuum that only the German army could have filled. After Versailles, however, the Allied powers would not have tolerated a "military" Germany.

Yet the army, as the only real power in Germany, tolerated the Weimar government only grudgingly, while individual units and officers actively sabotaged it. Hitler infiltrated the fledgling Nazi party as an unofficial agent of the Bavarian army command before taking the party over. There was no scarcity of "political" generals acting on their own, but Hindenburg alone commanded wide respect, and, as president of the Weimar republic, he saw himself as a caretaker and hoped, to the end, for the return of his Kaiser. But Hindenburg was forced to appoint Hitler as his chancellor in 1933, and when the aged general died one year later, the last constitutional brake on the Nazis died with him.

Those issues are recalled in some detail because many people are still convinced that economic disorder played a major part in the rise of a dictator whose territorial ambitions then led to World War II, and they fear that economic disorders might produce similar results now, even if on a lesser scale.

However, the horror experienced by Europe and the world during the first half of the twentieth century can be viewed more accurately as a war fought with an interval from 1914 to 1945, to fill the vacuum left by the disintegration of the Austro-Hungarian empire. Those events had economic consequences rather than causes. It does not follow that economic disorder is free of political dangers, but only that it does not automatically entail such dangers, and it can, in some cases, have an opposite and benign effect, as in the recent restoration of some democracy in Argentina and a moderation of excessive cruelty in Chile.

The run-up to present debt difficulties

During the past decade, commercial banks provided about half the net financing needs of the non-oil-developing countries. The loans helped cover the countries' current deficits plus additions to their reserves (Table 7, page 65). Commercial bank lending was concentrated on about a dozen advanced developing countries in Latin America and Southeast

Asia, which were only marginally dependent on foreign official flows for their external financing. Investment and economic and export growth during the 1970s were exceptionally high in the regions where those borrowers are concentrated. During the decade, real annual economic growth averaged 8 percent in Southeast Asia and 6 percent in Latin America, compared with 5.6 percent in the world's 102 broadly defined developing countries and 3.2 percent in the industrialized countries of the OECD.

According to World Bank estimates, real export growth was also exceptional among the major market borrowing countries. During the 1970s, Korea's exports rose by an average of 23 percent a year in real terms, Mexico's by 13.4 percent, Chile's by 10.9 percent, Argentina's by 9.3 percent, and Brazil's by 7.5 percent. By comparison, that growth rate was 5 percent for all developing countries and 3.3 percent for the mature industrialized countries of the OECD.

Despite heavy borrowing, rapid export growth kept the ratio of debt service to export earnings below the generally accepted "safe" level of 15 percent for countries such as Indonesia, Korea, Malaysia, and Venezuela. But by 1981, debt service ratios had risen above 50 percent for Brazil and Chile and to around 35 percent for Mexico and Argentina, a warning of the difficulties ahead.

The steep rise in the cost of borrowed money, especially of borrowed dollars, was a major contribution to those gathering difficulties. The World Bank has estimated* that a single percentage point change in short-term dollar interest rates had an annual impact of more than $1.2 billion on the combined net debt service of Mexico, Brazil, and Argentina, the three largest market borrowing developing countries, by 1981–82.

From 1979 to 1981, the foreign interest payments of those three countries rose by $10 billion, or 170 percent, and the interest payments of the thirteen biggest market countries among the LDCs rose by $18 billion, or 165 percent. At the same time, the value of world trade began to decline in 1980 and dropped further through 1983. The accompanying erosion of world oil prices affected some major market borrowing countries like Mexico, Venezuela, and Nigeria, while Argentina encountered special difficulties as a result of the South Atlantic war with Britain in the early spring of 1982. Although banks continued to lend to heavily indebted countries almost to the end in the hope of averting a crisis, the pressures were building inexorably. By 1982, the dollar values of developing countries' exports were plunging, while the interest cost of their debt continued to rise.

**World Debt Tables 1982–83* (Washington, D.C.: International Bank for Reconstruction and Development, February 1983).

7 • The crisis breaks

The crisis broke suddenly on August 20, 1982. The Mexican government abruptly proposed a moratorium on $19.5 billion of principal payments, which the government and its agencies were due to make to about 1,400 commercial banks during the remainder of 1982 and in 1983. Events moved with dramatic speed. The Mexican government quickly agreed to meet with a committee of bankers appointed to negotiate on behalf of all foreign creditor banks. The U.S. government provided $1 billion in prepayment for oil imports from Mexico. Bridging finance of $925 million was provided for up to one year by the U.S. Treasury, which was matched by the Bank for International Settlements, pending the agreement of an adjustment program with the International Monetary Fund.

The Bank of England, the Federal Reserve System, and other central banking authorities acted immediately to persuade larger international banks and, through them, regional and smaller banks to maintain credit lines to Mexican banks in the international interbank market. Jacques de Larosiére, the managing director of the IMF, informed creditor commercial banks that new complementary financing on their part would be a condition of IMF assistance to Mexico, as it later became for Brazil and several other countries (on the little-publicized precedents of complementary financing required from the banking system by the IMF when it agreed to adjustment programs with Togo in 1980 and with the Sudan in 1981).

Mexico was only the first of a number of heavily indebted countries to take this route. By mid-1984, thirty-five developing and East European countries had interrupted full debt service on about $120 billion of external debt, but even then there was still considerable uncertainty among debtor countries, their creditors, central banks, and international agencies about the precise totals involved. (The breakdown provided in Table 1 represents no more than the best estimates available at mid-1984. Those estimates, however, are good enough for all practical purposes, although not, of course, for those directly involved in the continuing renegotiations.)

Of the approximately $120 billion on which full service has been interrupted since the summer of 1982, only about $12.7 billion consists of debt owed by the governments of the borrowing countries to the governments of Western donor countries. The far bigger portion consists of debt owed by governments, their agencies, and private sector borrowers to private foreign creditors, including international companies, but mainly international commercial banks. The amount of debt to commercial banks on which full service has been interrupted was officially estimated at more than $90 billion by the end of 1983, equaling about half the gross and about 60 percent of the net foreign banking liabilities of the countries concerned.

The grand total of about $120 billion consists of international debt whose original terms have been renegotiated since mid-1982 or which were still under negotiation in the first half of 1984. The total includes repayments of principal due to have been made in 1982, 1983, and 1984, which have been stretched out for six to eight years. In addition, it includes more than $20 billion of short-term debt originally incurred for up to a year, which was consolidated into medium- and longer-term obligations. Beyond that, the grand total includes some arrears of principal and interest payments.

The breakdown confirms the overwhelming concentration of debt-servicing difficulties among a few of the biggest market borrowers in the developing world. Almost half the debt on which full service has been interrupted is owed by Mexico and Venezuela, about another quarter is owed by Brazil, Argentina, and Poland. Almost 20 percent of the remaining quarter is owed by six other countries, Chile, the Philippines, Yugoslavia, Rumania, Peru, and Ecuador. Thus more than 90 percent of the external debt restructured or being restructured is owed by only eleven borrowing countries, while more than twenty other countries account for the residual.

Put another way, nearly 70 of the World Bank's broadly defined 102 developing countries were still servicing their international debt in full in 1984, including such major market-borrowing countries in Asia as Korea, Malaysia, and Taiwan. Almost two years after the Mexican shock, debt difficulties were still confined to a minority of borrowing countries. There has not been, so far, a generalized "debt crisis."

The role of borrowing governments

The spate of recent international debt renegotiations has thrown into sharp relief the roles played by governments, international agencies, central banks, and commercial banks. And it has shown that their ability to manage events is limited.

Although global economic trends made a large contribution to current international debt difficulties, inefficiency on the part of the governments of some borrowing countries also played a part. Sound management of external debt is an important responsibility of governments in borrowing countries, and a majority of developing countries were able to keep up their external debt service despite growing difficulties after 1979.

The prerequisite of sound debt management for borrowing countries is information. Governments of borrowing countries need constant information on the total amount, the currency composition, the interest terms, and the maturity profile of outstanding public and private sector foreign debt. They need such information before they can even begin to project their borrowing and debt-servicing capacity on the view they take of the volume and price trends of their exports and imports, and the view they form of the trends of international exchange and interest rates.

Information on foreign debt incurred without government guarantees by companies in the private sector is particularly important. Government failures to collect sufficient information on a growing volume of such private sector international debt contributed to the foreign exchange scarcity that forced several major borrowing countries to interrupt full external debt service from mid-1982. But only 18 of the 102 broadly defined developing countries that report their medium- and longer-term international debt to the World Bank report international debt incurred by their private companies. Of course, in many developing countries, the private sector is small, and its foreign debt is nonexistent or insignificant. The private sector foreign debt of some of the biggest market borrowers among the developing countries is, however, extremely large, and yet many of those governments, for example, the Mexican and Argentinian, were among those that kept very little track of such borrowing.

The collection of prompt and adequate debt information poses political, not merely technical problems. Official information-collecting departments must have sufficient authority as well as competence to collect information from ministries and nationalized industries, and they must feel free to present the full facts, palatable or otherwise.

International agencies have found a close correlation between borrowing countries with poor debt-reporting systems and those that run into external debt-servicing difficulties. The need for information goes deeper than the requirements of debt management. Governments need accurate information about their external debt structure when formulating economic policy, which also must take into account the trend and deployment of domestic savings and the extent to which those savings can be augmented, if at all, by external borrowing.

When difficulties occur, several courses of action are open to the governments of borrowing countries. The abrupt approach of the Mexican authorities struck many observers as excessively dramatic and even brutal at the time, but as efficient in retrospect. The prompt arrangement of bridging finance from the U.S. government, the Bank for International Settlements, and the commercial banks that were persuaded to maintain credit lines to Mexican banks was accompanied by the imposition of exchange controls intended, among other objectives, to ensure equal treatment for all foreign creditors. Mexican companies paid the peso equivalent of their external debt service into special accounts with the Mexican central bank, which then assumed the foreign exchange liability to foreign creditors.

Broadly speaking, the Mexican approach was adopted by Argentina and Peru, while Chile, Venezuela, Uruguay, and Poland followed more closely the Brazilian approach. The Brazilian government moved slowly. It sought to win creditors' confidence by a protracted round of informal international discussions and by hesitating to interfere with market forces, such as in the interbank market where lines to Brazilian banks were being rapidly eroded even before that country's difficulties came into the open.

Although Brazilian banks began encountering difficulties in the international interbank market as early as August 1982, no official announcement was made until late October, and even then it promised a formal approach to the International Monetary Fund for conditional assistance only after the elections to Brazil's federal Assembly in November. Throughout the latter part of the year, the governor of Brazil's central bank toured foreign financial centers trying to raise new, additional financing without much success. It was only at the end of December that the Brazilian authorities first invited the representatives of foreign banks to discuss the country's problems, and external debt service was not suspended until January 1983. The efforts to avoid the suspension were well intentioned, but it proved far harder to restore interbank lines to Brazilian banks once they had eroded than it was to maintain those lines to Mexican banks.

The road taken by Mexico and the almost opposite choices made by Brazil are not the only options. The Yugoslav government approached the International Monetary Fund in 1982, and the IMF then informally approached Yugoslavia's creditor banks acting, in this case, as a catalyst to get negotiations started rather than in its customary and more public role of a catalyst in the adjustment process. Hungary avoided restructuring by informally asking the IMF in 1981 what kind of economic program it might recommend if asked. It then adopted as its own a program on the lines suggested by the IMF, enabling Hungary to go attracting foreign capital with the renewed confidence of the markets.

8 • The role of official agencies

The Bank for International Settlements, in Basle, founded in 1930 to handle the funding of German war reparations and then the restructuring of foreign debt by Germany, Austria, and some East European countries, has periodically supplied first aid in emergencies. Its members consist of the central banks of the United States, Japan, and most West and East European countries (excepting the U.S.S.R.). The BIS has evolved into a forum where central bankers and bank supervisors try to harmonize their policies and actions.

The BIS, which had previously provided bridging finance to some member countries pending their agreement on adjustment programs with the International Monetary Fund, assumed an expanded role by offering bridging finance on an unprecedented scale to nonmember countries like Mexico, Brazil, and Chile in 1982 and 1983. The BIS has provided bridging finance, guaranteed by its member central banks, for up to a year. However, the president of the BIS, Fritz Leutwiler, said in the summer of 1983 that the BIS might not have sufficient resources to provide bridging finance in all cases.

The BIS's reluctance to commit itself to a bridging role may have been reinforced by the postponement of several repayments by the Brazilian authorities in the spring and summer of 1983. The BIS announced, helplessly, at each postponement that it would not, for the present, call the guarantees of its member central banks. Although Brazil did then clear its debt to the BIS, that experience left the international institution more wary about its first aid function.

In addition, the BIS gives commercial banks and the public an ever improving flow of information on the terms and structure of international bank lending worldwide, as reported to it by the central banks of the main financial market countries, which in turn obtain their information from the commercial banks in their jurisdictions.

The International Monetary Fund is commonly described as the "catalyst" in the adjustment process, although that description might have been applied equally to its earlier role as the monitor of a pegged exchange rate system. It is the international equivalent of a credit union. Member countries subscribe according to their means, and they may draw in relation to their subscriptions.

The IMF's 147 member countries are entitled to draw an initial tranche of their entitlements without any conditions, but after that they are required to meet increasingly stringent conditions for the management of their economies to qualify for further drawings in their "higher" credit tranches. The IMF provides medium-term finance, commonly for three to five years and, occasionally, for up to ten years. But the sums it lends are not as important as the conditions that have to be met; meeting them helps bring the current deficits of troubled member countries under better control, making them eligible once again for market borrowing. Under the pegged exchange rate system, the object of agreements with the IMF was to underpin the fixed exchange rate. Under the present regime of floating exchange rates, the objective is not essentially different, because the aim remains that of helping to achieve economic recovery.

Before the emergence of a chain of international debt difficulties following the Mexican moratorium of August 1982, the U.S. administration argued that an enhanced role for the IMF was not synonymous with a substantial enlargement of its resources, because the Fund's conditions matter more than the relatively small sums it actually lends. The U.S. Congress took a similar view when it hesitated before approving, in November 1983, increases in the IMF's resources, which had been agreed to by the United States and other member governments almost a year earlier. The "conservative" view, taken to its extreme, holds that the IMF could function without any resources of its own, as commercial credit rating agencies do. And, logically, that argument is irrefutable. However, a majority of its members, including the United States, took the view that the IMF must have some funds of its own to lend if it is to win the acquiescence of member countries for often harsh economic adjustment programs. It remains true, however, that the IMF's seal of approval matters more than the financial assistance it provides.

The IMF serves, also, a useful public relations purpose because it allows member governments to blame the hardship of adjustment programs on distant and allegedly hard-hearted bureaucrats in Washington. Of course, the staff of the IMF merely gives formal expression to changes of conduct that borrowers themselves would need to adopt to keep or regain the confidence of their creditors (a point subtly taken by the Hungarian authorities in the case cited earlier).

The World Bank, formally known as the International Bank for Reconstruction and Development, while actually the world's biggest single development agency, has now also assumed a crisis function. Its membership of 144 countries is almost identical to the IMF's. The Bank, again like the IMF, was created in 1944; its soft-loan affiliate, the International Development Association, in 1960. By the end of their 1983 fiscal year, the Bank and IDA had lent about $120 billion for about 3,500 projects in more than 100 countries, and nearly 40 percent of the projects financed by the Bank and IDA attracted some complementary financing from regional development banks, donor governments, and commercial banks.

Although the Bank group has traditionally concentrated on financing infrastructure, like roads, dams, harbors, and hydroelectric systems, it has also provided funds to raise productivity in member countries by investment in health, education, and a growing proportion of "structural adjustment loans." The object of such loans is to help borrowing countries restructure their economies to achieve a more sustainable balance of payments after three to five years. The loans are intended to anticipate and avoid economic crises through economic reforms and changes in investment priorities. For instance, a "structural adjustment" loan may be used to help a country dismantle special protection of its industries to make them more competitive in domestic and world markets.

The World Bank approved a package of special measures in February 1983 to help resolve the international debt-servicing difficulties of the developing countries. It temporarily lifted its ceiling limiting structural-adjustment lending to 30 percent of any country's total borrowing from the Bank. It agreed to increase high-priority lending, especially for investments that were likely to increase the export earnings of borrowing countries, and decided, also, to accelerate disbursements of loans already approved. The Bank estimated that during its two-year special program, through mid-1985, gross lending would be increased by $2 billion, or 8 percent more than previously planned, and that its net lending would rise by 25 percent (disbursements less debt service).

The role of central banks. The central banks of the major industrial countries have come to play a growing part in several ways. One, already mentioned, was to guarantee bridging finance provided by the Bank for International Settlements in 1982–83, including $1,450 million to Brazil, $925 million to Mexico, $500 million each to Argentina and Yugoslavia, and $300 million to Hungary (which, in Hungary's case, helped avoid the interruption of external debt service).

Some central banks, notably the U.S. Federal Reserve System and the Bank of England, put what was authoritatively described as "heavy pressure" on banks in their jurisdictions to maintain or restore interbank credit lines to the banks of troubled debtor countries, especially Mexican and Brazilian banks. However, because other central banks, such as those of Germany and Switzerland, did not put similar pressure on their commercial banks, the efforts of the American and British monetary authorities were not wholly successful. Although they helped persuade their commercial banks to maintain interbank lines to Mexican banks, they were unable to persuade the banks to restore reduced lines to Brazilian banks. That experience has caused some central banks to reconsider risking their credibility in the future by attempting more suasion than they can feel confident of exercising. A conciliatory approach to creditor banks proved more successful when Paul Volcker, the chairman of the Federal Reserve Board, Anthony Loehnis, an executive director of the Bank of England, and William B. Dale, then deputy managing director of the IMF, helped convince commercial banks that it was in their own interests to provide a second medium-term financing package of $6.5 billion to Brazil, in December 1983 (following a $4.4 billion syndicated loan agreed to, after far greater hesitation, in February 1983).

A more fundamental expression of commitment to the stability of the international financial system by the world's leading central banks is contained in a statement promising that they would act jointly as lenders of last resort in case of need. The statement, first made in September 1974 (two months after the collapse of Germany's Herstatt Bank), was publicly confirmed as remaining in force by Christopher ("Kit") McMahon, deputy governor of the Bank of England, in May 1982. The statement said that the Group of Ten* central banks ". . . are satisfied that the means are available for the provision of temporary liquidity to the Euromarkets and would be used if and when necessary." But the statement deliberately refrains from spelling out in advance the precise circumstances and the scale on which such liquidity might be provided, in the classical tradition of not undermining market discipline by defining actions that might be taken by lenders of last resort. In that connection, the statement said, "It would not be practical or advisable to lay down in advance detailed rules and procedures for the provision of such liquidity" to the Euromarkets in case of need.

There is still some ambiguity, also, over the Basle "concordat" of 1975, refined in June 1983, under which a growing number of central banks and supervisors informally agreed, within the forum of the BIS, on a division of responsibility for the supervision of international banking. The "concordat" holds that the authorities of a bank's parent company assume the main responsibility for supervising its foreign branches, while the authorities of the host country assume the principal responsibility for supervising foreign banking subsidiaries in their jurisdictions. The Office of the Comptroller of the Currency, responsible for supervising

---

*United States, Japan, Germany, France, Britain, Italy, Canada, the Netherlands, Belgium, and Sweden. Since 1962, they have periodically lent supplementary resources to the IMF for relending by the Fund under the General Arrangements to Borrow. Switzerland, which had been associated with the Group of Ten, from the first, agreed in 1983 to become a member of the GAB.

federally chartered banks in the United States, and the New York State Banking Commission both have resident staffs in London to help the Bank of England supervise U.S. branch banks and American banking subsidiaries in the United Kingdom. In addition, U.S. bank supervisors regularly visit U.S. banks in other leading financial centers. However, the "concordat" concentrates narrowly only on supervision, specifically exempting central banks and other supervisory authorities subscribing to it from any responsibility for acting as lenders of last resort. In other words, it divides responsibility for supervising international banking, but it does not allocate responsibility for remedying any setbacks that might occur in spite of joint supervision. That "gap," however, is inevitable because some of the supervisory agencies, for example, America's Comptroller of the Currency, are not central banks and cannot therefore act as lenders of last resort.

The events of 1982–84 provide evidence that the extensive international central banking cooperation to cushion financial shocks was largely effective. That does not justify complacency and, to some extent, is deliberately intended not to. The vagueness of the central bankers' 1974 statement is partly deliberate, so as not to erode the market's self-discipline. Beyond that, however, some questions remain. For example, since central banks did not adopt a uniform approach during the debt-servicing difficulties that emerged after mid-1982, would they act equally to provide liquidity to the Euromarkets if that proved necessary?

9 • International debt restructuring

The mechanics

The approach adopted toward the unprecedented international debt renegotiations from the summer of 1982 was based on experience gained during other debt restructurings. Commercial banks, particularly American commercial banks, drew on their long experience of corporate debt restructuring (a routine but relatively unpublicized part of banking). Because the American banking system is not centralized, medium- and longer-term corporate lending in the United States tends to be syndicated among numbers of banks under the leadership of one or a few, a practice adopted by the Eurocredits market from its beginnings in the early 1960s.

International market debt, like corporate debt that needs restructuring in the United States, is renegotiated with the help of steering or advisory committees of large commercial creditor banks, nearly always the same groups of banks that acted as loan syndication leaders in the first place. U.S. commercial banks have had a prominent role in committees renegotiating Latin American foreign debt, while European and especially German banks have taken a similar leading position in renegotiating loans to Eastern Europe.

Debtor countries and creditor banks have been able to draw also on experience gained during more than twenty-five years of debt renegotiations between governments in the "Paris club" and the restructuring of sovereign debt to commercial banks, which began to complement relief agreements between governments from the mid-1970s.

The Paris club, in which developing countries negotiate the restructuring of public sector debt owed to the seventeen governments of the Development Assistance Committee* of the OECD, traces its origins to the restructuring of some Argentinian official debt in 1956. The club

*The members of the DAC are Australia, Austria, Belgium, Canada, Denmark, Finland, France, Germany, Italy, Japan, the Netherlands, New Zealand, Norway, Sweden, Switzerland, the United Kingdom, the United States, and the Commission of the European Communities.

came into being as an informal negotiating forum because debtor and creditor countries wished to establish common terms and conditions for restructuring applications, instead of attempting more complicated bilateral negotiations. Debtor and creditor countries have met, from the first, at premises provided by the French Treasury, which also supplies a chairman, at present Michel Camdéssus. Creditor countries, however, resisted for years any suggestion of a standing forum, for fear that such an admission might encourage more relief applications and, for the same reason, hesitated until 1974 before appointing a small secretariat.

The club, which operates on the basis of experience and precedent, has no formal rules. A standard approach and some fairly rigid procedural rules have, however, evolved since the mid-1970s. Creditor governments met on their own from the beginning to decide the merits of relief applications, and they still do. Although they began by relying on their own judgment of whether debtor countries were making sufficient efforts to bring their external payments under better control, that task has been assigned to the International Monetary Fund since the mid-1970s.

The Paris club meets to consider restructuring applications only after the applicant country has first agreed on an IMF economic adjustment program that entitles it to the use of IMF conditional upper credit tranche financing. Once an IMF program has been agreed and a restructuring application accepted for consideration, an oral presentation is made by the debtor country in Paris, explaining the causes of its problems, the measures being taken to remedy them, and the terms of relief being sought. Representatives of the IMF discuss the economic adjustment policies already adopted, representatives of the World Bank evaluate the country's longer-term development strategies and prospects, and representatives of the United Nations Conference on Trade and Development attend as "friends of court" for the applicant country.

Relief has been mainly confined to the restructuring of repayments of principal falling due within a "current" or consolidation period of up to two and a half years, including repayments of principal due at the time at which debt relief is requested. Repayment of principal is commonly allowed to be stretched out over eight to ten years, the first half of which is usually conceded as a grace period during which no principal repayments are required. However, creditor governments usually insist that interest payments be uninterrupted and, moreover, at a "moratorium rate," a market-related rate of interest that is usually, but not always, above the rate of interest at which the official loans were originally provided.

Over time, Paris club agreements have come to include provisions intended to secure equal treatment for all creditors. The agreements now require that countries obtaining relief from DAC governments try to restructure also the debt they owe to non-DAC governments and to private creditors, including commercial banks. Debtor countries must try to restructure debt to such creditors on terms no more favorable to those creditors than the terms agreed with the DAC, but that requirement is not met in all cases. Nevertheless, the requirement did lead to some market debt renegotiations to complement DAC restructurings from the late 1970s. Since 1982, that process has been reversed in some cases, when debtor countries first negotiated new terms with their bankers and then approached the Paris club (i.e., Brazil and Mexico).

Another development is the evolving compromise between debtor countries seeking longer-term relief, which would allow them time to make "structural" adjustments in their economies, and the consistent view of creditor governments that relief should be given only for the shortest period needed to allow debtor countries to adjust as promptly as possible to "liquidity" difficulties.*

The compromise that has come into being between debtor and creditor governments is embodied in the "goodwill clause" under which creditor governments undertake to consider favorably, but without any commitment, further requests for relief in succeeding years for as long as a debtor country continues to meet the targets of its IMF adjustment program in full. New restructuring is considered only for debt not previously the subject of relief. The requirement making further relief dependent on the meeting of adjustment targets incorporates the principle on which the IMF itself disburses successive tranches of conditional assistance it has agreed to provide to a member country.

The "goodwill clause" of Paris club agreements is an admission of the difficulty faced by all creditors and borrowers, which consists of discovering the fine point between conditions too lax to induce sufficient adjustment, or too harsh to be met. The result in either event is failure, leading to yet another round of renegotiations, as is evident from the number of recidivists who have returned to the Paris bargaining table three, four, or even five times. The "goodwill clause" recognizes that reality, and, like all evolutionary approaches, it has merits. First, it expresses in a practical way a reconciliation of differences of interest more acceptable to all concerned than the alternatives of endlessly repeated negotiations, default, or repudiation available at any given point. Second, arrangements that have evolved out of past experience may logically evolve further out of fresh experience.

Until 1978, commercial bank debt restructuring agreements linked for-

*The period over which a short-term "liquidity" difficulty becomes a longer-term "structural" difficulty equals the length of a piece of string.

mally to Paris club reschedulings (or agreements that informally took place about the same time) were confined to countries that were only marginally indebted to the banking system. That pattern was first broken with the renegotiation of a large part of Turkey's debt to international commercial banks in 1979. But it was only in 1982 that countries heavily indebted to commercial banks restructured their banking debt without first approaching the Paris club. Poland led the way, followed by Mexico, Brazil, and others.

Up to the late 1970s, commercial banks renegotiating international debt tried to confine themselves to "refinancing." The term is now loosely used, but then it was more narrowly defined to mean the provision of new money that would allow countries in difficulties to go on servicing existing debt while making the necessary economic adjustments. This had the advantage of allowing creditor banks to go on classifying all such lending, old and new, as "performing loans" producing a stream of income. Rescheduling, or restructuring, meaning the granting of new terms for servicing existing debt, was long resisted by creditor commercial banks.

Even during the time when they confined themselves to a narrowly defined "refinancing" of international debt, commercial banks required debtor countries to show that they were making economic policy changes to bring their balances of payments under better control. However, commercial banks did not try to formally suggest or impose economic adjustment policies on troubled debtor countries until 1976, when the government of Peru was asked to submit proposals for an adjustment program to its foreign bankers, who then disbursed the financing in two tranches to ensure that Peru was implementing its planned program.

Two years later, another change took place, again involving Peru. This time, breaking with their precedent of confining themselves to "refinancing," commercial banks agreed to allow the principal repayments Peru was to have made from the second half of 1978 to 1980 to be stretched out over six years. However, mainly as a result of implementing new economic programs, Peru found itself able to repay principal in a shorter time than covered by that restructuring, and took the opportunity to obtain fresh money at less than the penalty lending margins applying to the stretched-out repayments of principal.

Throughout their negotiations with troubled debtor countries, commercial banks have tried to resist consolidating arrears of principal repayments, the consolidation of short-term into medium- and longer-term debt, the restructuring of interest payments, and the consolidation of interest arrears. Since 1979, however, banks have felt obliged to compromise in all those respects in renegotiations with Turkey, Nicaragua, Togo, Poland, the Sudan, and others.

Banks have been particularly unhappy about the tendency to consolidate short-term trade financing, originally provided for up to a year, into medium- and longer-term debt. More than $20 billion of short-term international debt was consolidated in this fashion in 1982–83, locking banks into far longer positions than they had originally taken. Regional and smaller banks were especially resentful of such consolidations, and they became unwilling to maintain interbank lines to the banks of troubled debtor countries or even to maintain trade-related credits to such countries.

The renegotiation of international debt has slowly evolved beyond new financing (or "refinancing") to allow for uninterrupted service of existing obligations. Although such new financing is still provided, commercial banks have come to accept the stretching out of repayments of principal, consolidation of principal payments in arrears, interruptions of interest service, consolidation of interest arrears, and consolidation of short- into medium-term debt. But two forms of international debt have continued to be serviced in full.

The first, which has been and is likely to remain sacrosanct, is debt owed to the World Bank. The Bank's own funds are raised exclusively by the sale of World Bank bonds to institutional and individual investors in the world's leading financial markets. The Bank's capital, subscribed by member countries, exists for one purpose alone, which is to protect the bondholders. In order to raise money on the world's bond markets at the finest terms, the Bank has built up a prime credit rating. It has not lost a cent since it began lending in 1946, and its profits have been consistent and growing since 1948.

To keep its credit standing, on which its very existence depends, the Bank has an inflexible policy of not tolerating *any* deviation from the terms agreed upon when it provides a loan. Every borrower knows that the Bank would instantly call it into default if it failed to service its loans promptly and in full; moreover, under cross-default clauses, any borrower called into default by any creditor is at once declared in default by all creditors to ensure an equitable divison of assets. This unwavering policy gives the World Bank the status of a privileged lender, which is perceived as being in the interests of all, because the World Bank depends on its special status to go on lending, and its lending then attracts finance from other creditors.

A second class of creditors, whose claims have so far been serviced in full, do not have equal assurance of special status. These are the investors in bonds issued by developing and some East European countries. A proposal that debt owed to bondholders should be reconstructed alongside debt owed to commercial banks was defeated by only a single vote of the advisory committee of thirteen commercial banks responsible for renegotiating Mexico's international debt in 1982. The narrowness of the vote made clear that holders of international bonds can no longer assume a specially protected status with the same assurance as before.

Although the sums raised through the sale of international bonds by developing countries are far smaller than the amounts raised on the wholesale Eurocredits, or medium-term bank loan market, those sums are not negligible. In the five years through 1983, developing and East European countries raised about $16 billion on the international bond markets, including $6 billion issued by Mexico alone and another $2 billion issued by Brazil and Venezuela. In the secondary markets, prices of outstanding bonds of developing countries fell sharply in early 1983, pushing yields on such bonds to double the yields obtainable on bonds of comparable maturities issued by prime borrowers like the World Bank and the European Investment Bank. And, despite some recovery later in 1983, LDC bonds were still yielding about 50 percent more than comparable maturities of other borrowers, providing starkly visible risk premiums.

Improving the process

A number of proposals have been made for underpinning or improving the international lending system at its vulnerable margin. It is easiest to deal first with those that seem to hold the least promise. Among them are a number of proposals for official guarantees of international bank loans, or schemes that would allow banks to sell their restructured international claims at a discount. The proposals are that such guarantees or discounting facilities might be offered by the governments of the major Western countries through their central banks or some other agencies.

Such proposals, however, raise several questions. An underlying risk is that, if national authorities acted individually to guarantee or discount the international lending of their banks, each country might do so on different terms. The result would be the financial equivalent of the undeclared trade war that has evolved through the competitive subsidization of export credits. An international initiative to provide guarantees or discounting facilities would avoid that risk, but the negotiation of international guarantees or discounting facilities might prove impossible to achieve in the absence of a crisis (as in the case of Henry Kissinger's proposed OECD "safety net"). And it might prove equally impossible during the stress of a crisis, a crisis being defined here as a growing accumulation of repeated international debt renegotiations.

There are other questions. If official guarantees are priced or official discount rates set at market levels, commercial banks might have limited inducement to pay for the guarantees or to take advantage of the discounting facilities. Moreover, any price would almost certainly be passed on to borrowers by being incorporated into the terms on new or restructured loans, so that borrowers would not visibly benefit either.

Alternatively, if the price, or insurance premium, charged for official guarantees is pitched below market levels, or if discounting facilities are offered on subsidized terms, the electorates of creditor countries may resist. Banks might be reluctant to face such resistance, or to pay for it by some loss of their independence. The difficulties encountered in 1983 in persuading the U.S. Congress to approve America's share of enlarged resources for the IMF suggest the obstacles that might be faced. The amount of money the Congress was asked to approve for the IMF was hardly large, at less than 1 percent of federal budget expenditures.

From the standpoint of borrowing countries, official discounting by the governments of creditor countries also might be unattractive, whether at subsidized or market rates. Creditworthy borrowing countries, which have avoided interrupting international debt service, would resent officially subsidized guarantees or discounting facilities that blur the distinction between borrowers. In the case of official guarantees or discounts at market rates, weaker borrowers would dislike a publicized measure of their credit rating (as in the case of bond yields), although that might usefully help spur them back to creditworthiness.

None of this argues against the discounting of international bank claims through private initiative in the markets, which has begun on a modest scale. Banks did periodically sell off some of their international medium-term international loans to other banks even before the present debt difficulties emerged. Private discount markets are unlikely to grow quickly to a size that would enable them to absorb anything more than the international claims of some regional and smaller banks, but even that much is marginally useful.

A modified approach

A far stronger case can be made for a modified approach to the renegotiation of international debt under medium-term restructuring and adjustment plans spanning periods of up to five years. Creditors, whether governments or banks, might then commit themselves to allow principal repayments falling due in each successive year to be stretched out, provided only that the borrowing country continues to meet its economic and balance-of-payments targets. The conditionality would provide the sanction. The rewards of returning to good credit standing and access to new capital on the finest terms as soon as possible provide their own inducement to borrowers in any case. The World Bank was converted to the medium-term approach in 1983, the IMF the following year* and, in May 1984, Western banks did, in fact, sign a three-year agreement covering $1.7 billion of Polish debt.

The strongest argument for a medium-term approach is that it would reduce pressure on troubled borrowers to achieve "instant adjustment" by concentrating narrowly on import reduction. That is precisely what a large number of developing countries did in the wake of debt-servicing difficulties, or to avoid such difficulties (Tables 8 and 9). In the two years through 1983, the dollar value of the imports of non-oil-developing countries fell by 17 percent, and the average fall in the case of oil-exporting LDCs was 16 percent. Even countries in good credit standing reduced their imports (like Hong Kong and Singapore). Others kept the growth of their imports well below the levels of earlier years (like Saudi Arabia and Korea). At the extreme, Mexico and Nigeria cut their imports by nearly 60 and 70 percent, respectively, over the two years, partly reflecting heavy overspending at an earlier stage.

Since developing countries as a group account for about 30 percent of the value of world trade, severe, simultaneous, and protracted import reductions on the part of the biggest trading countries among the LDCs would undermine the global economic recovery necessary for an orderly return to full debt service. The risk for developing countries is losing imports needed for making manufactured exported goods. The risk for the industrialized countries is that the developing countries provided markets, in 1982, for more than 45 percent of Japan's exports, more than 40 percent of America's, more than 30 percent of Italy's, and almost 30 percent of the exports of Britain and France.

Another risk incorporated in the "quick fix" of narrowly concentrating on import reduction is that it cannot be sustained. Moreover, there is a danger that import reduction may take place at the expense of more fundamental and lasting economic adjustment, which involves removing impediments to the most efficient allocation of resources within debtor countries.** Such fundamental adjustment includes the removal of tax distortions, subsidies to producers and consumers, and various forms of indexation "against" inflation (which merely institutionalize inflation), as well as the abandonment of artificial exchange rates (which simply promote hidden capital outflows through the familiar routes of

**World Debt Tables 1983–84* (Washington, D.C.: International Bank for Reconstruction and Development, January 1984), p. xxi; *International Monetary Fund Survey,* June 18, 1984, p. 177.

**On the part of industrial countries, such adjustment includes opening their markets more freely to imports, especially from LDCs.

overinvoicing imports and underinvoicing exports). Even when pursued with determination, such adjustment programs take time to work.

At a lesser level, the medium-term approach to restructuring reduces the exhausting demands of repeated negotiations on a limited number of senior public servants and international bankers. That becomes especially true when a seemingly continuous renegotiating circuit is set in motion, as it has been since mid-1982. The precedent for the medium-term approach being argued here exists in the "goodwill clause" of Paris club agreements: creditors undertake to consider favorably, but without commitment, future relief applications as long as the borrowing countries are meeting their adjustment targets. It does not seem a large step to give the commitment from the start and to make relief in successive years dependent on the meeting of annual targets, thus avoiding yearly negotiations.

Constructive compromises

Any widespread move toward the possibly greater efficiency of a medium-term approach to international debt renegotiation would involve, however, some compromises from lenders and borrowers, and such compromises would be feasible only because they would be in the interests of both.

First, any move toward the medium-term approach to restructuring would prove realistic only if borrowers once again confined themselves to renegotiating the stretching out of principal repayments. Interruptions of interest service cause special concern to banks and bank supervisors by downgrading assets into the class of "nonperforming loans"; even though such loans sometimes produce a larger flow of income than performing loans.* Inclusion of short-term debt in relief packages makes banks reluctant to maintain trade credit lines to countries that urgently need to trade in order to return to full debt service. Such consolidation

*The U.S. Comptroller of the Currency classifies four categories of "problematical" loans, the first two consisting of loans that need special watching because of their potential weaknesses. A third category consists of loans requiring corrective action, and the fourth consists of loans producing no income. "Nonperforming loans," defined as those on which interest is overdue ninety days or more, are fitted into any category from one through four, depending on the perceived likelihood of a resumption of full service. Some nonperforming loans in fact pay interest, though irregularly, at above-market rates and thus produce a high if unreliable stream of income. Loans written off are not invariably lost; at least part of the principal is often recovered after time.

of short- into medium- or longer-term debt is therefore partly self-defeating for countries and their creditors.

Lenders, especially commercial banks, have exhibited some willingness to consider the advantages of a medium-term approach over the past year or so, although some remain reluctant to state that openly for fear of setting a dangerous precedent (their reluctance is comparable to that of the Paris club's delay in acknowledging its existence). At the same time, it is clear that a medium-term approach is linked partly to the question of penalty-lending spreads and fees. The impact of international debt renegotiations on banks has been partly cushioned in the past few years by a stiffening of restructuring terms. In 1978 and 1979, principal was still being restructured over five to six years, with two years of grace and at penalty margins of 1.25 to 1.5 percent above the banks' cost of money, as measured by Libor, or the London interbank offered rate for dollar deposits. However, some of the 1982–83 restructuring agreements, including those with Mexico and Brazil, provided for stretch-out periods of up to eight years, but still with only two and a half years of grace, at penalty lending margins of up to 2.5 percent above Libor, plus penalty restructuring fees of up to 1.5 percent. Those lending margins compare with lending spreads of less than 1 percent obtained by Brazil until 1980, and as little as 0.5 percent available to Mexican borrowers as late as June 1982.

The penalties compensate banks for the very fine terms they felt obliged to concede in the borrowers' market that prevailed during much of the 1970s and into the early 1980s. If arrangement fees are taken into account, a large part of recently restructured debt is earning banks about 2 percent a year more than the terms on which most of that debt was originally contracted. Moreover, during the grace periods, the penalty margins apply to the total of restructured debt outstanding because none of it is being run down during those years. On one, admittedly rough, calculation, it was estimated in 1983 that international commercial banks were earning about an extra $1.75 billion a year on the $90 billion of international bank debt then recently restructured or in the course of renegotiation.*

Such additional earnings give banks more scope for providing against interruptions of full debt service and possible losses. But the imposition of penalty fees and spreads runs counter to common practice in the restructuring of domestic corporate debt, when bankers are willing to concede easier terms for a time to help tide companies through a dif-

*Group of Thirty, "Commercial Banks and the Restructuring of Cross-Border Debt," New York, 1983.

ficult period. However, that difference between common practice in restructuring corporate and sovereign debt merely underscores the well-known distinction between companies, which can be liquidated, and countries, which cannot. It is an open question whether penalty spreads on renegotiated international debt speed or impede the return of borrowers to full service. Some bankers are now suggesting that a progressive reduction of penalty spreads might provide a further inducement to countries climbing back to full credit standing.

The "rational" scenario

So much for a rational scenario. It is one in which troubled debtor countries and their foreign banking creditors grope, perhaps slightly more tidily over time, toward resolutions that are in their common interests. However, debt difficulties can be resolved in this way only if sustained and uninflationary economic growth in the leading industrial countries continues and if international trade barriers do not go on proliferating.

Even following a rational scenario, the outcome would be less than perfect. Some international debtors would take longer than others to return to full external debt service. A minority, in terms of money owed, might not return to solvency at all. They are the private corporations in debtor countries that may go bankrupt as a result of governmental constraints placed on domestic demand as part of the adjustment programs designed to make their countries creditworthy again.

Western commercial banks will go on earning a stream of income on "nonperforming" loans (sometimes a higher income than on their performing loans), but so long as those loans are classified as substandard, neither the banks nor their supervisors will be confident that the loans will continue to be serviced. Some debt, notably the international debt of some private sector borrowers in troubled countries, may have to be written off. Even then, the creditors may eventually recover a part of that debt, as creditors often do on claims they have formally written off.

In that best of all possible worlds, costs will fall on all. The shareholders of some Western banks will lose money, and the taxpayers of some Western countries will pay indirectly to the extent that banks are able to write off such losses against their tax liabilities. A far greater cost will have been imposed on individuals the world over by the slowdown in economic growth caused by those official policies that culminated in the global monetary disinflation of 1979–82. But, in that best of all possible worlds, the progression to new and sunlit uplands will already have started.

It sounds too good to be true, and probably is. Although Western monetary policy has laid the basis for a resumption of uninflationary economic growth, it cannot by itself ensure that such growth will be sustained. All the major Western countries, except Japan and the United Kingdom, are at present trapped in structural budget deficits, which include a large element of fixed costs that are not sufficiently reduced by a cyclical economic upturn, generating an increase in tax payments with a fall in unemployment and other social outlays. It is the intractability of those budget deficits, rather than the deficits in themselves, that has paralyzed fiscal policy. At root, a resolution of that flaw requires a direct confrontation of the deeply seated conflicts of interest within societies, which find expression in the gap between what electorates want and what they are willing to pay.

In the absence of some progress toward more manageable and flexible fiscal policies in the West, an economic upturn will not be sustainable because corporations will not invest in new plant or new service industries unless they can rely on a steady economic expansion—but that requires the investment in the first place. Of course, it is not wrong to hope for a steady growth of the world economy, but it would be prudent to take into account the possibility of a continuation of growth by fits and starts, in the familiar "stop-go" cycle. And, at worst, there is the possibility of an economic collapse, in which case the financial system may still be saved because central bankers, as lenders of last resort, can print all the money they want. What they cannot do is to keep fully alive the world's "real economy," which produces jobs, goods, and services fulfilling human needs, but would not go on doing so in exchange for worthless money. In that worst of all possible outcomes, the international debt of a handful of developing and Eastern European countries will not be an important factor. What, however, if the debt difficulties of a few countries should become the proverbial final straw?

10 • Repudiation and default

Speculating whether debtor countries may repudiate their external debt or default is futile, but discussing how such developments might occur may be helpful.

The starting point is a clarification of terms. Any debt not fully serviced in strict accordance with the conditions on which it was provided is technically in default. It is up to the creditor to call the debtor into formal default, or to renegotiate the terms of the debt. The latter is the route that has so far been chosen by international creditors. Repudiation, on the other hand, is a course taken by the debtor alone.

The one country that is technically better placed than any other to repudiate its international debt and that has, periodically, repudiated large parts of that debt is the United States. Most international debt is denominated in U.S. dollars, including America's own liabilities to foreign creditors. That gives American governments unique powers to wipe out a part of America's debts worldwide, through inflation. This unique ability of American governments to write down international debt denominated in American currency (whose creation the American authorities control) greatly troubled President de Gaulle in the 1960s, and he tried, ineffectually, to guard France against the consequences by physically transferring France's national reserves of gold* to Paris from New York and London.

From 1970 to 1980, the effective or weighted average exchange rate of the dollar fell by 20 percent, according to the IMF, against the currencies of America's major trading partners. Since foreign claims on the U.S. government and its residents rose by about $1,200 billion during that decade, the effect was to wipe out, or repudiate, about 20 percent of that debt, the equivalent of about $240 billion, or about twice

---

*The gold has proved almost useless, particularly in the short run. There are about sixty years of gold production above the ground, about half of it concentrated in the central bank vaults of six Western countries, among which France is the fourth-biggest holder (after the United States, Germany, and Switzerland). France has run down its gold stock by almost half, but it took nearly twenty years of careful marketing to do so.

the amount at stake in today's international "debt crisis." In practical terms, that process of silent repudiation meant that nonresidents who lent to the United States or invested in it during the 1970s lost 20 percent of their claims on the United States in "real" terms, as measured by the volume of American goods and services to which their claims entitled them.

Then between 1980 and 1984, the average dollar exchange rate recovered more than all the ground lost in the preceding decade. Repudiation and reparation to foreign creditors through debasement and restoration of domestic currency is not, however, a course that can be taken by countries other than the United States, except, on a far more limited scale, by other countries issuing currencies also used for international investment and reserves, namely, Germany, Japan, Switzerland, Britain, and the Netherlands.

The kind of repudiation envisaged in today's international debt difficulties involves either the "mad dictator" who attempts the dramatic gesture of liberating his country from the shackles of world finance, or governments that might feel themselves driven to a last resort by intolerable domestic political pressures. The possibility cannot be dismissed, if only on the ground mentioned in the introduction, that no eventuality can ever be ruled out entirely. It seems unlikely, however, because the costs of repudiation are far higher than those of servicing external debt in order to go on trading with the world. A few small and poor countries could turn inward, as Albania has long done, but in doing so they damage their own people rather than the world. A few small countries of special strategic value to larger allies can rely on being underwritten, as they have been, because the amounts are small enough for the major powers involved to hide them in their budgets in ways that make them nearly invisible to legislators. For example, Costa Rica has the worst record of debt service in Central America, but also happens to be the most peaceful country in the region and therefore the only one not kept afloat by foreign military aid.

If any larger debtor country attempted repudiation, it would find it very difficult to maintain trade with the rest of the world, except by some form of barter with powerful political allies, who would exact a far higher price than aid-donating governments and the commercial banking system.*

---

*Since the pure coincidence of exact reciprocal need rarely occurs, barter tends to consist of complex sets of transactions, which the use of money efficiently bypasses. In that process, "protector" governments have sometimes tended to make generous allowances in their own favor (e.g., the U.S.S.R. in its dealings with Cuba and Eastern Europe).

There remain, of course, some options. One is the repudiation by a new government of some of the "unacceptable" portions of foreign debt incurred by its predecessor. Another consists of what Dubliners mean when they say that you may commit any sin you wish, provided you do not call it by its name; that is de facto repudiation, or default by attrition, a road pursued by at least one Central American country whose debt to foreign banks has been restructured annually for several years. The amount is negligible for the world banking system and small even for the country's creditor banks. A new renegotiation takes place each year after the country fails to meet in full the restructuring terms agreed upon a year earlier. The time involved stretched senior management capacity at the creditor banks, which then delegated the annual renegotiations to less senior personnel. The process, if continued, would represent repudiation of at least a part of the country's international debt in all but name. Some of the larger creditor banks would gladly write off their claims on the country, excepting for their fear of the precedent they might create.

Yet that course is open only to smaller countries, and they pay for it in the form of little new external finance for their trade and development. It is a degeneration of the debt-restructuring process, and one that could be handled more efficiently within the medium-term approach suggested earlier, in which the disbursement of new funds is automatically halted to a troubled debtor country not meeting its adjustment targets. That control over disbursements is precisely the way in which the International Monetary Fund ensures the continuing implementation of programs agreed upon with borrowing member countries.

A more realistic danger is that some creditor might, at some stage, set in motion the process by which a debtor country is called into formal default by all its creditors. Self-interest, rather than pressure from their governments, would deter larger international banks from taking the first, irreversible step. A smaller bank might not be similarly restrained by self-interest or official pressure; for example, a small American bank, with a claim on, say, the Mexican government, could go to court to obtain seizure of a Mexican-government-owned airliner berthed at Kennedy Airport. The moment that happened, every bank and other creditor around the world with a claim on the Mexican government would have no alternative but to join the scramble for any Mexican assets subject to seizure anywhere abroad, including Mexico's externally held bank balances. Thereafter, the creditors would launch an avalanche of lawsuits against each other to ensure a fair division of the assets available, and the international banking system would find itself recycling lawyers' surpluses in the way it used to recycle oil surpluses. There might be little that the governments of the major powers could do once such a scenario unfolded. The job of the major Western governments is to create conditions in which no such thing happens.

Governments of the world's leading countries are responsible for creating a stable framework for the world economy. Debtor countries that have mismanaged their own economies are forced, by the act of borrowing beyond their means, to bring their balances of payments under better control. As the jargon has it, they are obliged to adjust, and there is nothing like having no money to encourage adjustment. In that mundane environment, troubled debtor countries and their creditors will soldier on from day to day. Such is the way of the world.

Tables

Table 1

International Debt Renegotiations, 1982–84[a]
(in billions of dollars)

Country	Market Debt	Paris Club	Total	Percentage of Total
Mexico	37.0	2.0	39.0	
Venezuela	18.4	0.0	18.4	
Brazil	9.8	3.8	13.6	
Argentina	12.0	0.0	12.0	
Poland	5.7	0.0	5.7	
	82.9	5.8	88.7	74.0
Chile	4.1	0.0	4.1	
Philippines	4.0	0.0	4.0	
Yugoslavia	3.8	0.0	3.8	
Rumania	2.5	0.7	3.2	
Ecuador	2.8	0.2	3.0	
Peru	2.4	0.5	2.9	
	19.6	1.4	21.0	18.0
Nigeria	1.6	0.0	1.6	
Morocco	0.0	1.2	1.2	
Costa Rica	1.0	0.1	1.1	
Uruguay	0.7	0.2	0.9	
	3.3	1.5	4.8	4.0
Other Countries[b]	1.0	4.0	5.0	4.0
Total	**106.8**	**12.7**	**119.5**	**100.0**

Source: Compiled from unpublished European and other international official estimates, mid-1984.

a. Market debt is owed mainly to commercial banks; Paris club debt is owed by developing countries to the seventeen donor governments of the Organization for Economic Cooperation and Development.
b. Includes twenty other countries.

Table 2

Troubled Debtor Countries Ranked by Gross Market Debt Outstanding, End–1983

Countries that renegotiated debt, 1982–84
(in billions of dollars)

	Unguaranteed bank debt	Guaranteed debt	Total
1. Mexico[b]	60.8	6.6	67.4
2. Brazil[b]	54.5	11.4	65.9
3. Argentina	22.9	3.3	26.2
4. Venezuela	22.0	1.7	23.7
5. Poland[b]	10.0	5.4	15.4
6. Nigeria	6.3	5.9	12.3
7. Chile	10.9	0.8	11.8
8. Yugoslavia	8.0	3.5	11.5
9. Philippines	7.1	2.8	9.9
10. Panama[a]	7.1	0.5	7.7
11. Liberia[a,b]	6.0	0.6	6.6
12. Peru[b]	4.4	1.3	5.8
13. Morocco[b]	3.0	2.1	5.1
14. Ecuador[b]	4.0	0.8	4.8
15. Rumania	3.4	0.9	4.3
16. Ivory Coast	2.5	0.9	3.4
17. Zaire[b]	0.6	1.2	1.8
18. Uruguay	1.6	0.1	1.7
19. Cuba[b]	0.8	0.7	1.5
20. Jordan	0.4	1.1	1.5
21. Sudan[b]	0.8	0.6	1.4
22. Costa Rica[b]	0.7	0.1	0.8
23. Zambia[b]	0.3	0.5	0.8
24. Bolivia	0.5	0.2	0.7
25. Senegal[b]	0.3	0.4	0.7
26. Jamaica	0.3	0.3	0.6
27. Nicaragua	0.5	0.1	0.6
28. Madagascar[b]	0.2	0.3	0.5
29. Dominican Republic	0.2	0.3	0.5
30. Niger[b]	0.3	0.1	0.4
31. Togo[c]	0.1	0.2	0.3

Table 2 (continued)

	Unguaranteed bank debt	Guaranteed debt	Total
32. Malawi[b]	0.1	0.0	0.2
33. Guyana	0.1	0.0	0.1
34. Uganda[c]	0.0	0.1	0.1
35. Central African Republic[c]	0.0	0.0	0.0
Totals of above	**241**	**55**	**296**
Total for 154 borrowing countries	**523**	**135**	**658**

Sources: Organization for Economic Cooperation and Development, *External Debt of Developing Countries,* April 1984, and Bank for International Settlements -Organization for Economic Cooperation and Development, *Statistics of External Indebtedness,* July 1984. Unguaranteed bank debt consists of liabilities to banks in the United States, Japan, Canada, and twelve European reporting countries, plus U.S. branch banks in the Caribbean and Far East. Guaranteed debt consists of liabilities to those reporting banks plus other creditors, mostly multinationals, in the form of trade credits insured by twenty member governments of the OECD.

N.B.: 119 borrowing countries were servicing foreign debt in full at mid–1984. Rounded figures do not add in all cases. 0 = negligible.

a. Data for Liberia and Panama exclude interbank liabilities as well as credits for shipping registered in those countries under "flags of convenience."

b. Renegotiations with the Paris club as well as the banking system.

c. Renegotiations with the Paris club only.

Table 3

The Growth of International Bank Lending*

(in billions of dollars)

End of	Claims of BIS Reporting Banks on: Industrial Countries	OPEC	Non-oil LDCs	Eastern Europe	Total
1977	405	39	97	38	590
1978	530	56	120	48	770
1979	660	64	156	56	950
1980	790	70	193	60	1,130
1981	920	72	230	61	1,310
1982	1,005	79	247	53	1,420
1983	1,048	90	261	50	1,449

	Proportion of Total BIS Reporting Banks' Claims on: Industrial Countries	OPEC	Non-oil LDCs	Eastern Europe
1977	69	7	16	6
1983	73	6	18	3

Source: Bank for International Settlements, *International Banking Developments,* July 1984. Lending as reported to the BIS by banks in the Group of Ten leading industrial countries plus Austria, Denmark, Ireland, and Switzerland.

*Table excludes offshore centers in Bahamas, Cayman Islands, Hong Kong, Panama, and Singapore. Totals exclude unidentified lending. Some rounded figures do not add. BIS data *include short-term lending at up to one year,* unlike data from the Organization for Economic Cooperation and Development, which include only medium- and longer-term credits provided for beyond one year.

Table 4

New International Market Lending[a]
(in billions of dollars)

Year	OECD Countries	OPEC Members	Non-oil LDCs	Eastern Europe	Totals[b]
1972	13	0	3	0	20
1973	19	0	6	1	31
1974	26	1	8	1	41
1975	23	3	9	3	43
1976	38	4	13	2	63
1977	40	7	15	3	70
1978	62	12	27	4	111
1979	61	9	39	5	120
1980	74	7	30	3	121
1981	85[c]	7	49	2	150[c]
1982	122	9	37	1	179
1983	112	8	28	1	158

Source: Organization for Economic Cooperation and Development, *Financial Statistics, Monthly* (Part 1), August 1984.

a. Data for new international bonds and new medium-term bank loans. All figures rounded to $1 billion; 0 = less than $500 million.
b. Totals include also other borrowers, notably the World Bank.
c. Excludes $51 billion of credits provided to U.S. corporations to mount or repel mergers.

Table 5

New Eurocredits[a]
(publicized medium-term syndicated bank loans)
(in billions of dollars)

To:	1980	1981	1982	1983
OECD	41	47[b]	55	32
OPEC	7	6	8	7
Non-oil LDCs	28	41	32	25
Eastern Europe	3	2	1	1
Total	80	96[b]	96	67

Source: Organization for Economic Cooperation and Development, *Financial Market Trends*, various issues.

a. All figures rounded, and totals include some unclassified lending.
b. Excludes $51 billion of credits provided to U.S. corporations to mount or repel mergers.

Table 6

Lending Spreads on New Eurocredits
(in basis points)[a]

To borrowers in:	1979	1980	1981	1982	1983	1984[b]
OECD	62	59	58	56	64	62
Eastern Europe	70	88	62	103	112	69
OPEC	105	77	79	94	85	69
Non-oil LDCs	85	91	104	114	170	158
Average	79	74	80	77	114	117
Differentials of Non-oil LDCs over OECD	23	32	46	58	106	96

Source: Organization for Economic Cooperation and Development, *Financial Market Trends*, no. 28, June 1984.

a. A basis point equals one one-hundredth of a percentage point and is used for measuring changes in or differentials between interest rates. The lending spreads are those applying above Libor, the London interbank offered rate for dollar deposits. Most lending spreads are set above Libor for three- or six-month interbank deposits.
b. January to May.

Table 7

The Role of Banks in Financing Non-Oil LDC Current Deficits
(in billions of dollars)

	Financing Requirement (deficits plus changes in reserves)	Net Bank Financing	Banks' Contribution (percentage)
1973	21.7	9.8	45
1974	39.7	19.1	48
1975	44.7	23.2	52
1976	45.6	21.5	47
1977	41.4	16.2	39
1978	58.7	26.0	44
1979	73.6	36.7	50
1980	93.5	54.4	58
1981	109.8	54.9	50
1982	79.7	51.5	65

Source: International Monetary Fund, *Annual Report,* 1983, Table 10, p. 33.

Table 8

World Trade Changes, Exports
(percentage changes in dollar values)

	1981	1982	1983
Industrial Countries	-2	-5	-1
Oil Exporters	-8	-22	-19
Nigeria	-26	-16	-30
Saudia Arabia	+11	-33	-38
United Arab Republic	-2	-17	-17
Venezuela	+5	-18	-9
Non-oil LDCs	+4	-6	+2
Argentina	+14	-16	+1
Brazil	+16	-14	+8
Chile	-17	-3	+3
Mexico	+24	+11	0
Hong Kong	+10	-3	+5
South Korea	+22	+2	+12
Singapore	+8	0	+5
Philippines	0	-12	0

Source: International Monetary Fund, *International Financial Statistics,* various issues.

Table 9

World Trade Changes, Imports

(percentage changes in dollar values)

	1981	1982	1983
Industrial Countries	-5	-6	-2
Oil Exporters	+17	-1	-15
Nigeria	+26	-31	-43
Saudia Arabia	+17	+15	-8*
United Arab Republic	+10	-2	-5
Venezuela	+11	-5	-41
Non-oil LDCs	+7	-12	-6
Argentina	-10	-44	-17
Brazil	-4	-12	-20
Chile	+25	-45	-22
Mexico	+24	-39	-46
Hong Kong	+10	-4	+2
South Korea	+17	-7	+8
Singapore	+15	+2	0
Philippines	+2	-2	0

Source: International Monetary Fund, *International Financial Statistics,* various issues.

*Twelve months to June.